FOUR LECTURES

ON

THE WESTERN TEXT

OF

THE NEW TESTAMENT.

FOUR LECTURES

ON

THE WESTERN TEXT

OF

THE NEW TESTAMENT

BY

J. RENDEL HARRIS, M.A., D. LITT. (Dubl.)

FELLOW OF CLARE COLLEGE, AND LECTURER ON PALAEOGRAPHY
IN THE UNIVERSITY OF CAMBRIDGE.

WIPF & STOCK · Eugene, Oregon

Wipf and Stock Publishers
199 W 8th Ave, Suite 3
Eugene, OR 97401

Four Lectures on the Western Text of the New Testament
By Harris, J. Rendel
Softcover ISBN-13: 978-1-7252-9981-8
Hardcover ISBN-13: 978-1-7252-9983-2
eBook ISBN-13: 978-1-7252-9982-5
Publication date 2/4/2021
Previously published by C. J. Clay and Sons, 1894

"Nec sine voluptate audias eruditos viros, amicissime et jucunda verborum verecundia dissentientes, ut non disputationi quales re vera esse pleraeque solent, sed colloquio qualia veteres fingere consueverunt philosophi, interesse te putes."

J. D. MICHAELIS,
(*Curae in Versionem Syriacam*, 1755, p. 160).

PREFACE.

THE lectures contained in the following pamphlet are concerned with that problem of problems, the interpretation of the Western text of the New Testament. Since my tract on the Codex Bezae was published in 1891, there have been a number of weighty contributions to the solution of the problem, which have added much to our knowledge of the textual history of the New Testament, and made it necessary for me, before continuing my imperfect examination of the Cambridge MS., to estimate the results of the other workers in the same field.

The fact is there are now four separate and distinct theories before the world; Resch's theory[1] that the bifurcation in the primitive text of the New Testament is due to independent translations from a Semitic document (probably Hebrew); Chase's[2], that all the variants are due to reflexion from an Old Syriac translation; Blass's theory[3], that in the Lucan writings they are due to the issue of two separate drafts from the hand of the original writer—a statement which supports itself, in certain points, on a powerful programme of Peter Corssen, in which was demonstrated the antiquity and wide diffusion of that part of the Latin tradition of the text of the Acts which is in agreement with the quotations of Cyprian[4]; and my own,

[1] Resch, *Aussercanonische Paralleltexte.* Leipzig, 1892.

[2] Chase, *The Old Syriac element in the text of Codex Bezae.* Cambridge, 1893.

[3] Studien u. Kritiken, 1894, pp. 86—120, *Die zweifache Textüberlieferung in der Apostelgeschichte.*

[4] *Der Cyprianische Text der Acta Apostolorum.* Berlin, 1892. Corssen says some significant things about the modern edited texts, which he calls 'der destillierte Text, den die Modernen aus einigen griechischen Uncialen gewonnen haben,...nur ein Spiegelbild einer willkurlich fixierten Recension des vierten Jahrhunderts' (p. 24).

which claimed that there had been a reaction on the Greek text from the primitive Latin translations, as well as, occasionally, from the Syriac version. Further we have a remarkable chapter on the Codex Bezae in Ramsay's recent work *The Church in the Roman Empire*, in which numerous changes of the text are assigned to the hand of a Greek reviser acquainted with the geography of Asia Minor. I shall set my own theory for the present on one side, not because I have abandoned it, but merely remarking that my critics were probably right in saying that I had exaggerated the sphere of Latin influence, and I believe, equally right in conceding that a certain amount of Latinisation did exist.

The first lecture which discusses Resch's views was delivered more than a year ago, and printed in the Classical Review for June, 1893; it was not meant to be a final examination of Resch's theory, but merely to point out that a closer acquaintance on his part with the actual text of the Codex Bezae was necessary, and a consequent restatement of the arguments, before Resch was likely to meet with the exhaustive treatment, which I have no doubt his hypothesis deserves.

The other lectures are concerned chiefly with Mr Chase's theory that the Codex Bezae is under Old Syriac influence, and Dr Blass's view, that it is an original document, in good Lucan Greek.

Both of these writers have added much to the subject upon which they treat; and Mr Chase's is a theory, which in spite of certain peculiarities in its presentation, challenges the fullest scrutiny, and will certainly, if sustained, greatly advance the subject in hand. The lectures are, of course, an incomplete treatment of the questions at issue; but I feel hopeful that they, too, will do something to speed us towards the goal which the critics have been so long striving to attain, the complete explanation of the primitive variation and bifurcation in New Testament texts.

CREDNER AND THE CODEX BEZAE[1].

In a work just published, entitled *Aussercanonische Paralleltexte*[2], by Alfred Resch, who is already known to the world of Biblical criticism by his treatise on the Agrapha of the New Testament, will be found certain criticisms of my tract on the History of the Codex Bezae, which was published last year in the Cambridge *Texts and Studies*, just as Resch's researches are in Harnack's *Texte und Untersuchungen*. The parallel between our publications is not merely an external one, though I think it is fair to admit that we are distinctly imitating, in our little Cambridge series, the German research and enthusiasm which Harnack has done so much to crystallize : we are also working internally on parallel lines, and especially Dr Resch and myself are engaged on the very same questions, viz. the origin of the variant forms of the Gospels, only we are working from opposite ends; I am working up stream, and Resch is working down; I follow the readings of variant MSS. up stream until I find, as I suppose, their origin; Resch has divined, as he supposes, their origin and has only to read the facts in the light of his hypothesis; and we shall meet by and bye somewhere between our two starting-points, and it would be presumptuous at present to anticipate whether the meeting-point is nearer to my end of the line of action or of his.

But we may at least be grateful that each of us is able to appreciate the industry of the other, and not disposed unduly to depreciate the results which are brought forward; on my

---

[1] This Lecture was delivered in the Divinity School, Cambridge, Nov. 19, 1892.

[2] *Aussercanonische Paralleltexte zu den Evangelien: textcritische und quellencritische Grundlegungen*, von Alfred Resch. Leipzig, 1892.

side I am sure that this is the case, and I am confident that it is also true of Resch, for his newest work is charitable of my latest *brochure*, and charitable almost to a fault. Perhaps one reason for this, beyond the main reason of mutual charity which is happily spreading amongst Biblical critics, and in which Cambridge will always try to rival Leipsic, lies in the sense that Resch had that my researches, like his own, were as yet largely tentative and incomplete. Neither of us would wish to hurry the other to conclusions, or to prejudice work that is slowly maturing by an undue criticism of what has already been issued.

But we have come to a point where Resch judges my results to have suffered, from a deficiency in the preliminary manipulation of the data of the problem. Accordingly, as in the case of the excavators who cut the famous tunnel at Siloam, 'there is heard the voice of a man calling to his neighbour,' and it would be extremely discourteous on my part not to respond to the sound of the tools or the voice of the worker. Consequently, when Resch informs me, in a manner to which I certainly take not the least exception, that my results on the Codex Bezae will be vitiated by the neglect of the previous researches of Credner, and thinks it necessary for himself to restate the whole of Credner's position and many of his arguments, I feel it my duty to point out some of the reasons for my neglect of Credner, and to warn my fellow-labourer that, unless he is careful to work over all Credner's statements for himself, he will find that an earlier writer has digged a pit for his feet.

According to Resch, it became necessary for him to reproduce the fundamental lines of Credner's investigation of the Codex Bezae, because the latest discussion of the subject, in the Cambridge Studies, had not once alluded to Credner, to say nothing of giving him a proper attention. A re-statement of Credner's theory was, therefore, demanded; for Credner's was the most instructive investigation which the subject had received.

Credner detected three stages of development in the Codex Bezae: (i) the origin of the MS. lies somewhere in the second century, amongst Ebionite (Antichiliastic) Jews apparently in Palestine, and in its earliest form the text contained the Four Gospels, the Catholic Epistles, and the Acts of the Apostles. Two sources were employed in the production of the text, of which one is described by Credner as 'an unknown authority' or 'an Apocryphal Gospel.' The earliest form of the text was characterized by free handling and by numerous glosses (especially in the Gospel of Luke and the Acts of the Apostles).

The next stage of its development, or at all events the next stage which can be clearly made out, is dated by Credner about the year 500; the MS. tradition still lies within the circle of the Judaeo-Christian Church, but about this time an attempt was made to give the text a form more suitable for ecclesiastical use, by adopting the method of arrangement in sentences which Euthalius had introduced, somewhere about A.D. 480, and perhaps the Greek text may have been already paralleled by the accommodation of a Latin translation, similarly divided to the Greek. The ecclesiastical lections, which are marked on the margins of the Codex Bezae, must have been already attached to the text, for amongst them are 26 lessons for the Sabbath, which intimate Judaeo-Christian origin and usage; moreover, since they are in Greek only, it is unlikely that, at the time of their introduction, the Latin text had been attached to the Greek.

The third and last stage of textual development belongs to the end of the sixth or beginning of the seventh century, when the actual Codex Bezae was produced, by dictation of the sentences to a skilled calligrapher; the work was probably carried out in Southern Gaul, whither the text had been carried by some Oriental Jewish-Christian. The liturgical notes, which were in the copy from which the Codex Bezae was taken, had become defective through time and use, and were copied, by another hand to that of the calligraphist, in their worn and mutilated form. The Latin text was of course transcribed at the same time.

Such, in brief, is Credner's theory, as stated by Resch. And we must add that Resch not only states the theory but that he endorses it, referring the reader for the detailed proofs to

1—2

Credner's *Beiträge zur Einleitung in die Biblischen Schriften,*
pp. 452—518. It is true that Resch points out a weakness in
Credner's work, in that he did not recognize sufficiently the
relations between the Codex Bezae and the Old Latin and Old
Syriac texts, which constitute with it a distinct textual family.
But I think we may say without injustice that Resch, with this
single exception, endorses Credner's investigation and its
results. For instance, the view that the MS. has a Judaeo-
Christian origin is endorsed[1]; the 'unknown authority' of
Credner, which lies at the back of the Western text as one of
its sources, is identified with a secondary translation of the
original Hebrew Gospel[2]; and the stages of development which
Credner indicates for the Western text, as we find it in
Codex Bezae, are accepted and tabulated[3].

[1] *E.g.* p. 33. 'Hatte der Redaktor jenes Archetypus, jenes ältesten Evangeliencanons, ohne selbst Judenchrist zu sein, die—auch von Justin getheilte,
vermittelnde Stellung dem gemässigten Judenchristenthum gegenuber zum
Ausdruck gebracht, sofern er das judenchristliche Evangelium an die Spitze
dieses im Uebrigen echt katholischen Evangeliencanons gestellt hatte, so ver-
danken wir speciell die weitere Ausbildung der Handschrift, die uns jetzt im
Codex Bezae vorliegt, *ausschliesslich judenchristlichen Kreisen*, welche die
Apostelgeschichte und die katholischen Briefe, nicht aber das paulinische
Schriftthum, der Handschrift einverleibten. Auch die weitere Conservirung
der Handschrift im Laufe der nachsten Jahrhunderte wird, wie Credner ganz
richtig gesehen hat, *auf dieselben judenchristlichen Kreise* zuruckzufuhren sein.
Denn wahrend in der orthodoxen Kirche in Folge der canonischen Textrecension
die Exemplare jener vorcanonischen Evangeliensammlung langst verdrangt und
verschwunden und nur in Uebersetzungen erhalten waren, blieben *diese judenchristlichen Kreise* von der Textrecension der Grosskirche beruhrt, und
konnten so ein griechisches Exemplar jener vorcanonischen Evangeliensammlung fur ihren gottesdienstlichen Gebrauch bewahren und in jene spätere Zeit
hinuberretten.'

[2] P. 144. 'Bei der Besprechung dieser wichtigen Handschrift .habe ich
bereits darauf hingewiesen, dass die aussercanonische Textrecension, mit
welcher speciell das Lucas-evangelium in diesem Codex auftritt, zu erklären sei
aus dem Einfluss einer Uebersetzung des Urevangeliums, verwandt derjenigen,
welche von dem ersten Evangelium benutzt worden ist, und dass eben hierin die
von Credner gesuchte "unbekannte Autoritat" zu finden sei, "auf welche die
kuhne Textrecension des Lucas-evangeliums nach dem Codex D sich stutze,
indem hieraus auch die zahlreichen scheinbaren Conformierung des Lucastextes
nach dem Matthaustexte sich erklaren."'

[3] P. 35.

'A. Archetypus.
Griechischer Evangeliencanon spatestens um 110.

It is further stated, in accordance with Credner's views ('hat Credner jedenfalls richtig bezeichnet'), that in the history of the origin of the bilingual text we must allow that the Latin text was added to the Greek as early as 500, in order to allow for such corruptions as have arisen from the interaction of the Greek and Latin upon one another. But before this time the tradition of the text involved many marginal annotations, such as the Ammonian sections, and apparently the Sabbath lections, while at the time when this redaction was made, the lections of Euthalius were introduced, and the stichometric division of the text. For we know for certain (according to Resch) that the stichometric division of the Acts is due to Euthalius. And it is natural to assume that if at this time (about 500 A.D.) the Latin text, stichometrically divided, were added to the Greek, the Latin text would remain free from the previously existing Greek annotations of a liturgical character. And it is these liturgical notes, together with their Sabbath lessons, which more than anything else (*mehr als alles Andere*) entitle us to refer the origin and use of the Western text to Judaeo-Christian circles, and enable us to approve Credner's suggestion that the text was brought into Southern Gaul, in its later form, by some Syrian Jewish-Christian, probably a trader, and that it was finally dictated to a scribe, not very well acquainted with Greek, towards the end of the sixth century.

It is sufficient to present this brief summary, to show that Resch has absorbed Credner's views almost without modification; and since he has rarely added any reason for their reception except, by reference and implication, the reasons already given by Credner, we are entitled to conclude that he

B. Evangeliencanon
mit Apostelgesch. u. kathol Briefen
vor 200.
C. Neue Redaktion von B,
Beifugung des lateinischen Textes,
um 500.
D. Letzte Abschrift des
bilingualen Codex
gegen Ende des 6. Jahrhunderts.'

considers those reasons to be valid, and not to need much further enforcement.

The best way to see the error which Resch has made in thus endorsing Credner will be to follow the method which I adopted in my tract on the Codex Bezae, viz. to begin with the marginal annotations.

On p. 27 Resch has copied the following marginal note from the Codex Bezae, and given an elucidation of it :—

$$
\left.\begin{array}{l}
\text{ΓΝΟCΜΑ} \\
\text{ρΙΤΟΥCΑ} \\
\text{ΤωΤΗC} \\
\text{ΑΚΟΥΝΙ} \\
\text{ΜΟΥ}
\end{array}\right\} = \left\{\begin{array}{l}
[a\nu a]\gamma\nu o\sigma\mu a \\
[\pi\epsilon]\rho\iota \ \tau o\nu \ \sigma a \\
[\beta\beta a]\tau o\nu \ \tau\eta\varsigma \\
[\delta\iota]a\kappa o\nu\nu\iota \\
[\sigma\iota]\mu o\nu
\end{array}\right.
$$

i.e. it is a lection for the Sabbath which precedes the Sunday after Easter, which is called the διακινήσιμος. And it is inferred that since the lectionary direction is given in this imperfect form, it must have been copied from a previous MS. in which the direction had become partly illegible [1].

In this Resch was simply following Credner, who had taken the lection from Kipling, and had remarked that 'in unsere Handschrift konnten die verstümmelten Worte aber nur dadurch gelangen, dass sie, Buchstabe für Buchstabe, aus einer andern Handschrift eingetragen worden sind, welche schadhaft geworden war, dergestalt, dass die Anfangssylben fehlten.'— (*Beiträge*, p. 500.)

The mistake made (for as we shall see presently the explanation is erroneous from stem to stern) was partly due to Kipling, who had printed these liturgical notes on the margin of his text, in the same type as the text. But Kipling did not venture to make the liturgical note coeval with the MS., as must be the case, if the theory is to hold that it was to be found in the tradition of the text at an earlier date than the Codex Bezae itself. What Kipling said of it was as follows

---

[1] 'Die liturgischen Randbemeikungen, welche durch den fortgesetzten Gebrauch des fruheren Kirchenexemplars defekt geworden waren, wurden in ihrer verstummelten Gestalt der neuen Handschrift von einer andern Hand einverleibt.'

(p. xv.): 'notae liturgicae,...non a prima quidem manu, at certe tamen, ut mihi videtur, ante saeculum septimum appositae,' and Kipling's statement was copied by D. Schulz (*Disputatio*, p. 10) in the words 'Haec glossemata antiquissima, si minus a primâ quidem manu, at certe ante saeculum septimum iamiam adscripta esse.' How then did Credner come to attribute an artificial antiquity to such a liturgical note? Obviously it was the incomplete form in which the note occurs, which suggested that it had been copied from a previous Codex. But in this Credner was misled by Kipling, and did not see that what Kipling was trying to reproduce was an annotation on the margin of a MS., where a part of the MS. had been cut away.

And it is unfortunate that Resch, who has read through the Codex Bezae, both in Kipling's edition and in the edition of Scrivener, did not see the mistake that Credner had made, nor correct it, either by Kipling's preface or by Scrivener's preface and annotations. If he will turn to Scrivener's edition, p. 450, he will find the following note:

423 b. ll. 11—15...αγνοσμα..ρι του σα...τω της...ακουνι... μου (*i.e.* διακινησιμου sive ἑβδομ. a', margine abscisso L etc.);

and if he will further turn to the preface of Scrivener (p. xxvii.) he will find conclusive reasons for dating this corrector (whom Scrivener calls L) *not earlier than the ninth century.* It is, to say the least, unfortunate that Resch had not taken the trouble to verify such an easy point as the date of an annotator.

What then becomes of Credner's Judaeo-Christian liturgical notes, which, according to Resch, *more than anything else,* lead us to believe that the Codex Bezae goes back to a Judaeo-Christian origin? Not only does it appear that this particular case, on which so much has been built, is a delusion; but the whole of Credner's remarks on the liturgical annotations in the Codex Bezae are at fault: first, they do not belong to the date to which Credner wishes to refer them; secondly, they have nothing to do with the Jews.

As Resch has challenged an appeal to Credner, to Credner he must go; but he must not go without the MS. or some trustworthy edition of its text. And if Credner wishes to carry these liturgical notes back into remote antiquity, or even to the time of production of the Codex Bezae or the century before that time, he must be met with a stern palaeographical negative. None of these annotations are as early as the ninth century, and some of them are as late as the twelfth. Consequently it is hard to regard Credner's study of the Codex Bezae as the most instructive that has yet appeared; it is unjust to Scrivener, to say the least.

The number of errors which Credner has fallen into in his account of these marginal hands is simply appalling. I shall give one or two instances, if only to justify myself for having neglected Credner.

Would any one believe it possible that a lection marked against Matt. xvi. 28—xvii. 9 with the words μεταιμορφος αυναγνοσμα could be interpreted in the following manner ?—

'Ich weiss das seltsame erste Wort nur aus eine Vermischung des Griechischen mit dem Lateinischen zu erklären. μεταμορφος soll heissen, eigentlich : μετὰ morbos. Das Eindringen Lateinischer Wörter in die Griechischen Sprache des gemeinen Lebens ist aus dem N.T. bekannt. Hiernach sollte der bezeichnete Abschnitt als Gebet und Trost für Kranke und Genesende verlesen werden, und dazu passt auch der 'Inhalt.' The lesson is, as the matter shows, the regular one for the feast of the Transfiguration (τῆς μεταμορφώσεως). The date of the annotation is, as before, of the ninth century, yet Credner does not hesitate to say (p. 505) 'auch der Umfang und die liturgische Beschaffenheit dieser Randbemerkungen führen uns auf Judenchristen.'

A more striking case still is in a marginal annotation attached to John v. 18; which reads

ЄΡΙΑΝΑΠΑΥ
ΑΜЄΝΟϹ

and is rightly given by Credner in the form περὶ ἀναπαυσαμένους. That is, we have here a church lection pro defunctis. But according to Credner, who wishes to find traces of Judaeo-Christian usage, we are to see in the words an allusion to those persons who rest on the Jewish Sabbath; for according to his

view (p. 506), 'Dies bezieht sich auf die Judische Feier des
Sabbathes, welche ἀνάπαυσις heisst. Joseph. *Antiq.* 3, 12, 3.
Derselbe *contra Ap.* 2, 2. Epiphanius *Haer.* 42, 3. Thilo,
Acta Thomae pp. 146, 223. ᾿Αναπαυσάμενοι sind folglich
diejenigen, welche den Sabbath nach Judischer Weise als
Ruhetag feiern. Die Absicht des Verfassers dieser Bemerk-
ung kann nun keine andere gewesen sein, als das Unrecht-
massige der Jüdischen Feier des Sabbathes auf Johannes v. 18
gestützt hervorzuheben u.s.w.' And it follows that, if the
allusion to those persons who rest on the Sabbath be attached
to the passage in which Christ is charged with breaking the
Sabbath, then we are in the circle where Jewish beliefs are in
process of being antagonised; that is, the text belongs to a
time when the Church is being withdrawn from its half-Jewish
state into one more distinctly Christian. All this pyramid-on-
apex-building depends on the curious interpretation which
Credner makes of the marginal reading. Nor does he stop
here, but realizing that the case was not dissimilar to the one
which we previously discussed, he maintained that the imperfect form in which the marginal note is transmitted is again
a case where marginal annotations have been taken from a
copy in which they had become partly illegible.

But, as before, the marginal reading, which is by the very
same hand, refers to lectionary usage of the ninth century;
the two missing letters have been cut from the edge; and the
lesson is the proper one to be read over the departed. And
the reason for the selection of the passage is to be sought, not
in any allusion to Sabbath breaking, but in the doctrine that
the 'Son quickeneth whom he will &c.' It is the more strange
that Credner should have missed the meaning, since he cites
lower down (p. 511) a Roman burial inscription in the form
Τόπος ἀναπαύσαιως ᾿Αμμονίου καὶ Εὐτυχείου θρέπτου. But
the fact is that very little which Credner wrote will stand an
appeal to the manuscript, and for this reason I am sorry that
Resch has endorsed so much of his work, and especially that
he has laid such stress on the demonstration of a Judaeo-
Christian origin which Credner detected in the marginal
liturgical annotations. A reference to Resch (p. 34) will show

that he has carried up to the date A.D. 500 the Ammonian sections, the pericopes for the Sabbath, the lections of Euthalius in the Acts, and the stichometry (= colometry) of the MS. Let us then see what Scrivener says on the subject of the Ammonian sections in the Codex Bezae. He tells us (*Cod. Bezae*, p. xx.) that 'The Ammonian sections, without the Eusebian Canons, are inserted in the side margin of Codex Bezae by a scribe whom we shall hereafter show to have lived several centuries later than this manuscript was written'; and again (pp. xxvi. xxvii.) 'it is evident from a careful comparison of the marginal numerals of the Ammonian sections with the great body of the liturgical annotations (written in thick, clumsy letters with ink of a purple hue), especially in the Gospels, that they are the work of one scribe, whom we shall call L....... A bare inspection of Facsimile Pl. iii. no. 12 will prove that L...... cannot be dated before the ninth century.' I suppose that Credner was here misled by Kipling's edition in which the Ammonian numbers are printed with the text, though Kipling did not assume them to be coeval with the MS.: and Resch must have followed Credner, though a reference to Scrivener would have kept him from this hydra-headed catalogue of errors. We have now disposed of the argument from the Ammonian sections, as well as that from the pericopes for the Sabbath (which are a mere relic of Gallican usage in the ninth century, as I think might have been gathered from my own modest little tract). We come next to the question of the lections of Euthalius in the Acts, which Credner, followed by Resch, carries back to the time of Euthalius, very nearly. Here again we are dealing with marginal references of a later date, by two separate hands of the twelfth century. I do not even believe that we can make out an identification of the lections with the Euthalian system; but, even if we could, there would be nothing gained, for no result follows from the marginal ascription of Euthalian lections in the twelfth century. And I am only sorry that Resch did not see that he was treading on the thinnest of thin ice in following Credner.

But, it may be said, the stichometry of the MS. is surely an integral part of the MS. itself; and while on the one hand it cannot be more ancient than Euthalius, who invented it; on the other hand it must be early, for the Codex Bezae was obviously transcribed from a copy similarly divided to itself. But neither can this be made out, for a reference to Euthalius' reckoning of the στίχοι into which he divided the text agrees closely with the conventional book-measure obtained by dividing the text into breadths of sixteen syllables. And even if it be argued that Euthalius *colified* (to coin a word) his text into short sense-lines as well as measured it, there is no proof that the Codex Bezae contains his system, and, as far as the Gospels go, the line division can be carried back much farther, probably into the second century. So that all the details of the description of the MS. which Resch characterized as 'most instructive' are shown to be errors, arising from an insufficient acquaintance with the MS. itself. But, further, Resch has (p. 34) adopted from Credner the theory that the Codex was written from dictation. There is nothing in this which bears closely upon the problem of origins; and yet, as I have been directed to study my Credner, and Resch gives no other evidence than what is found in Credner, it may be worth while to look at the instances, and see whether the palaeographical argument is a just one.

Credner gives ten instances of errors introduced by aberrations of the ear in a scribe writing from dictation. Most of these would be rejected at once by any one familiar with the copying of uncial texts : *e.g.*

Luke xvi. 26, D has πειcει for μιcει (written μειcει in early texts).

Luke vi. 20, D has ετιαρac for επαρac.

Acts vi. 5, 4, D has μεcoν coι for μενoν coι, where the eye has wandered two or three letters.

Acts iv. 29, D has read απειλαc as αγιαc, which is certainly a palaeographical error.

But what need to go further? for if these are copyists' errors, the scribe was reading the book for himself, and not writing from dictation. The only instance which Credner gives that has any verisimilitude is John xiv. 21, where ἐμφανίσω has been read as ἐνφωνήσω. But the human mind is quite capable of such confusions, without the introduction of a dictator.

It seems, then, that all the particulars of Credner's theory which Resch has taken over are invalid and unsustained by an appeal to the MS. We do not mean to say that Credner's theory of a Judaeo-Christian origin of the Western text is an impossible theory, or the closely related theory of Resch. Only the reasons which have been brought forward thus far are out of harmony with the palaeographical facts, and new reasons must be found. *Non tali auxilio nec defensoribus istis.* We have no wish to disparage Resch's work on the text, which is extremely interesting and may lead to some very important conclusions. Only we must ask him to neglect Credner, and to allow other people to neglect him, when they can show good reasons for doing so. There is too much interesting work on hand for us to be justified in spending precious time in correcting the multitudinous errors of a critic of the last generation. Probably it would also be wise of Resch not to lay undue stress on certain other points, which he has borrowed from Credner, in reference to the theory of the Canon; for they do not affect his new theory of Gospel origins, and may cause it to be unfairly discredited. I mean, to take an instance, the statement that the original Judaeo-Christian Canon contained only the Four Gospels, the Catholic Epistles, and the Acts: and not the Pauline Epistles (Resch, p. 33). We are all agreed that the *Codex Bezae* does not contain the Pauline Epistles, and we are also satisfied that it contains one page of a single Catholic Epistle (probably the last of three originally extant Epistles of John); but we are not agreed that Codex Bezae is the Canon, nor that it is a Judaeo-Christian or Petrine book. Surely it would be better to reserve our judgments in the case of a MS. which is imperfect in the middle and at the end, and of which we have not even the right to affirm that it existed without a companion volume.

It is fair to make this last suggestion, because Resch has made a mistake of this very kind with regard to the completeness of a MS. in his notes on the Codex Sangallensis (Δ), which he thinks may go back into a very early base, partly because it is bilingual, and partly because it is limited to the Four Gospels. It is quite true that the Codex Sangallensis does contain many very early readings, but, as to its limitation to the Four Gospels, it is well known that the companion volume containing the Pauline Epistles is extant, and is known in the critical apparatus by the sign G[paul], and to librarians as the Codex Boernerianus.

I have said nothing so far in defence of my own theory about the Codex Bezae. The reader of Resch's little book will see that my explanations are not considered adequate, and that there are many readings where Codex Bezae deviates from the Canonical text, which are not easily explained by the hypothesis of Latin influence. I think this is quite possible and have no objection to make, if Resch can establish his contention; for I hope to see my way some day to all necessary corrections and expansions of my first statement But perhaps I may remark that there are some weak spots in Resch's list, and in his deductions from them. For example, if it be true that the reading of D in Matt. x. 6 (ὑπάγετε for πορεύεσθε) cannot be due to any retranslation, as the words are wholly indifferent in meaning, why does it follow that in Luke ix. 57, where D reads ὑπάγεις for ἀπέρχῃ, we are entitled to infer that the Itala MSS. also must have had ὑπάγεις or ὑπάγῃς in the texts from which they were translated, because they now agree with Cod. Bezae in reading *ieris* (wenn nun alle Itala-Handschriften mit der Vulgata ieris lesen und also ὑπάγεις... voraussetzen)? Or perhaps the retranslation would be invalid in support of Harris' theory, but good when employed in demonstrating the unity and antiquity of the Western text, which, of course, I hold as strongly as Resch?

THE OLD SYRIAC TEXT OF THE ACTS[1].

Mr Chase's theory of the Western text is that the peculiarities of the Codex Bezae are due to retranslation from an Old Syriac version; and apparently to this cause only, since he states that the demonstration of the Syriacization of the Greek text excludes the theory of its Latinization, and I suppose would equally, from his point of view, exclude the theory of every other form of textual reaction and bifurcation. In other words, the hypothesis of re-translation from the Syriac is an adequate one to explain the peculiarities of the Bezan Text[2].

The hypothesis here presented is, in one sense, not a new one. It is, in fact, the theory of J. D. Michaelis in the last century and D. Schulz in the present century. Michaelis' statement is as follows[3]: "an alteration of the Syriac from the Latin cannot possibly be supposed;... in Syria, where Greek was understood, no man could have thought of correcting the Syriac Testament from a Latin translation, and those Syrians, who were acquainted with Greek, were undoubtedly ignorant of Latin....More probable is the supposition that the Syriac has had influence on the Latin, especially in those examples where an error is committed, that might happen more easily to the Syrian than the Latin translator. The Latin text is properly a composition of several ancient versions, one of

---

[1] This lecture was delivered in the Divinity School, Cambridge, January 19th, 1894.

[2] It even explains, from Mr Chase's point of view, the itacisms of the scribe ($\dot{a}\delta\epsilon\lambda\phi\eta$ for $\dot{a}\delta\epsilon\lambda\phi\omicron\iota$) and the Alexandrian verb-forms (as $\dot{\epsilon}\theta\omicron\rho\upsilon\beta\omicron\upsilon\sigma\alpha\nu = \dot{\epsilon}\theta\omicron\rho\upsilon\beta\omicron\upsilon\nu$ $\dot{\eta}\sigma\alpha\nu$). But we must not judge a theory by the extravagances into which it may lead its promoter.

[3] Marsh's *Michaelis*, Vol. II., part 1, p. 25.

which must have been made by a native Syrian[1], as appears
from the Syriasms found in the Latin text of several ancient
MSS., which greatly exceed in harshness the Syriasms of the
Greek Testament: this Syriac translator was probably guided,
in obscure passages, by the version of his own country, the
effects of which appear to be felt at this very day in the
Vulgate.... But the foregoing hypothesis is very insufficient
to account for that general coincidence observed between the
Old Syriac[2], the Old Latin, and those ancient Greek manuscripts, which were undoubtedly written in the West, as appears from the Latin translations with which they are accom-
panied. The wonderful harmony between the two most ancient
versions of the New Testament, one of which was spread
throughout Europe and the North of Africa, the other propa-
gated from Edessa to China, could have no other cause than
a similarity of the Greek manuscripts in the West of Europe
and the East of Asia, which must have deviated in an equal
degree from our printed text and the manuscripts of what is
called the Greek edition[3]."

From the foregoing it appears that Michaelis had attempted
to explain the Western readings by means of reactions from
the Syriac (and he refers his readers for further details of the
theory to his *Curae*, pp. 169—173), but that he clearly held
the theory very doubtfully, regarding it at best as a partial explanation, and that he settled down into what has been, since
his day, the accepted theory, that the Western readings are a
bifurcation in the primitive Greek text. Apparently he did
not exclude the idea of some Syriac reaction on the Greek;
for he says (Vol. I. p. 321), "It is not improbable that the
Syriac and Coptic versions have had some influence on the
Greek copies of the New Testament."

---

[1] This does not seem to agree with the previous statement that "those Syrians
who were acquainted with Greek were undoubtedly ignorant of Latin."

[2] By the Old Syriac, Michaelis does not mean what is implied in that term
to modern ears; he is speaking of the Peshito, in contradistinction from the
Philoxenian version.

[3] He means the Recensio Constantinopolitana of Griesbach (as Marsh
explains).

His commentator, Marsh, observes that Michaelis' theory would require that the Syriac version must have been made before the end of the first century (in order that it might be employed in the structure of the primitive Latin rendering): but he regards the premises as resting on very unstable ground, denies the necessity for supposing that a primitive Syriac version earlier than the Latin existed, or the probability that, if it existed, it would have been employed so as to colour the early Latin translations. No doubt the connexion between the Peshito and the Old Latin was not an easy one to establish[1]; nor does it seem that the attempt to forge the critical link between the two versions has been successfully re-attempted since the publication of the Curetonian fragments.

Now in what respect does Mr Chase's theory differ from the obscure and somewhat self-contradictory statements of Michaelis, or the suggestion of Schulz that the Codex Bezae has been under direct Syriac influence?

In the first place, it involves the substitution of the Old Syriac (in the modern sense) for the Peshito; this step was an obvious one, if the text of the Gospels was to be handled in the light of a proposed theory of Syriac reaction; for it is in the Curetonian fragments and in the recovered Tatian Harmony that we find those decisive proofs of the agreement between the ancient Eastern and Western texts, which was at first suggested by the comparison between the Peshito and the Old Latin versions.

But, in the second place, Mr Chase does not choose as the ground of his re-statement of the theory of Syriacization, the text of the Four Gospels, in which it was possible to reason from the Old Syriac of Cureton, and the Old Syriac quotations in Ephrem, Aphraates and other Syriac writers to the early Western text of the Codex Bezae and the Latins; but he chooses for his ground of debate the text of the Acts of the

---

[1] The support brought to Michaelis' theory by D. Schulz in 1827 (*Disp. de Cod. Cant.*) was not sufficient to bring the hypothesis into public favour or reception; it consisted chiefly in laying emphasis on coincidences in reading between D and the Peshito version Michaelis refers also to a work by Storr which I have not seen (*Observ. sup. ver. Syr.* Stuttgart, 1772).

Apostles, where, up to the present time, no evidence of an Old Syriac text has been forthcoming, and starts on his enquiry with the hypothesis that there once existed an Old Syriac version of the Acts. Such a hypothesis is, in his view, adequate to explain the Western readings which are so thickly strewn in the Bezan text of the Acts, which readings bear in themselves, according to him, the marks of derivation from a Syriac original.

The boldness of this hypothesis is evident; and it has naturally provoked opposition. The question is immediately asked, 'Why do you not test the theory of Syriacization in the Gospels where the Old Syriac does in great part exist [and we might add, where it has lately come to light in an almost complete form], instead of flying off in search of an Old Syriac text which is not yet known to exist?' Mr Chase's answer is two-fold; first, that he is especially interested in the text of the Acts; second, that the intrusive phenomena in the text which he has to explain are more decided in the Bezan Acts than in the Bezan Gospels. We might add that the wisdom of the choice of ground is also seen in the fact that we are in the Acts of the Apostles free from some of the disturbing factors which occur in the text of the Gospels; the assimilations of one Gospel to another do not obtrude themselves on the reasoning, and the probability of Aramaic elements in the sources (that death-trap for the man who is calculating Syriac influences) is, to say the least, much smaller in the Acts than in the Gospels, and may, perhaps, be entirely absent.

In this sense, then, the ground is wisely chosen; but what of the hypothesis, which is to explain the phenomena of the text, and to be accepted as a true hypothesis on the ground that it does so explain them? Naturally the first question that would be asked by a critic would be whether there was any tangible evidence for the existence of an Old Syriac version of the Acts of the Apostles; it ought to be possible, for instance, to demonstrate the existence of such a text, either from the quotations in the Homilies of Aphrahat, or from the works of Ephrem, or by making a scientific demonstration that either the Peshito, or the primitive form of the Philoxenian version, leans on an earlier text of which it constitutes the revision. Unfortunately no attempt seems to have been made either by Mr Chase or any one who preceded him to clear up these points. The five places where Aphrahat quotes the Acts do not furnish any satisfactory evidence on the point; not a single one of the 190 glosses which in my first studies I selected from the text of the Acts for special examination has, if we may judge from Tischendorf's apparatus, the attestation of either of the great Syrian fathers in question; and as to the known versions, we have not yet succeeded in getting behind the text of Thomas of Heraclea to that of his predecessor Philoxenus of Mabug, much less have we been able to analyze this important textual nucleus into its primitive parts: and it is the same with that imperfectly studied version, the Peshito.

It is, however, certain that an Old Syriac text of the Acts did exist, and that Mr Chase's hypothesis can be removed into the region of facts. We are in a position to prove that the Old Syriac text is, in a certain sense, extant, and has been before the public for more than half a century. The demonstration which we are going to give of the existence of this ancient text is of great critical importance, and while we must not conclude from the fact of the text's existence that it was necessarily the source of the Western variants it will certainly help us towards the final solution of the question.

Precisely as the commentary of Ephrem on the Harmony of the Gospels, which now attracts such constant study and is the centre of such lively critical interest, lay dormant in the Armenian text published by the fathers of the Monastery of S. Lazaro at Venice, until it was made accessible by the Latin translation of Mösinger, so have certain other works of Ephrem been blushing unseen and wasting their sweetness on what is, critically at all events, a desert air.

The first to be noticed amongst these translated works of Ephrem which the Armenian has preserved are his commentaries on the Pauline Epistles; which have, in the course of the last few months, appeared in a Latin dress, and so have become accessible to general criticism. As soon as the book appeared it was made the subject of review in three brilliant articles in the *Theologisches Literaturblatt* by Zahn, who had long ago petitioned for its publication in Latin[1].

Zahn pointed out the peculiar features in the commentary which identified it as a work of the same hand as had commented on the Diatessaron, and the peculiar features of the text which characterized it as belonging to what is called the Western tradition, and as being an older form of the Syriac than that which is found in the Peshito.

The most interesting of all the peculiar readings in the new text is perhaps the expansion of the anti-Judaic verses in Gal. iv. 21—27.

The text and commentary of these verses is as follows (we print them without distinction of type on account of the difficulty of distinguishing, in a text which has gone through some process of glossing, the commentary from the text).

Hae vero fuerunt symbola duorum testamentorum. Una populi Judaeorum secundum legem in servitute generans ad similitudinem eiusdem Agar.

Agar enim ipsa est mons Sina in Arabia; est autem illa similitudo huius Jerusalem, quia in subjectione est, et una cum filiis suis servit Romanis.

Superior autem Jerusalem libera est, sicut Sara; et eminet supra omnes potestates ac principatus. Ipsa est Mater nostra, Ecclesia Sancta, quam confessi sumus.

When we compare this passage with the current Greek text, or with the critical apparatus of the New Testament, there is not at first sight anything that suggests a very different text to the common text of the epistle; but when we turn to Tertullian's fourth book against Marcion, or to Zahn's reconstructed text of the epistle as used by Marcion, we find, to our surprise, that a large part of the apparent commentary is part of the text of Marcion; and since there is no reason for doubting Tertullian's tradition of this text, nor for supposing that Ephrem's text has had any connexion with a faulty interpretation made by Tertullian, we have no other alternative than to conclude that Ephrem is commenting on a Marcionized text.

[1] *Theol. Lit.-Blatt,* for Septr. 29, 1893 and two following weeks.

That this is really the case appears, as we have said, from the
language of Tertullian (*Adv. Marc.* IV. 4):

"unum a monte Sina in synagogam Judaeorum secundum
legem generans in servitutem, aliud super omnem principatum
generans, vim, dominationem et omne nomen quod nominatur
non tantum in hoc aevo sed et in futuro, quae est mater nostra
in quam repromisimus sanctam ecclesiam."

It will be seen that Tertullian's text, like Ephrem's, had
incorporated a passage from the Epistle to the Ephesians (i. 21),
describing the Church, in sufficiently bold language (but which
can be justified by a little interpretation), as seated, with the
Lord, far above all principality and power.   And the explanation is also added, both by Tertullian and Ephrem, that this
Upper Jerusalem who is our Mother is the Holy Church, whom
we have confessed.   True, Tertullian's text differs at first sight
in that it uses the word 'repromisimus'; but this may very
well have been due to a variant rendering of a primitive ὡμολο-
γήκαμεν, which may equally mean 'to promise' and 'to con-
fess[1].'

This remarkable passage then formed a part of Marcion's
text; it may well startle us as a textual phenomenon, not only
for its own sake as indicating a very free handling of the
biblical text for dogmatic ends, but also as containing a
reference to the Symbol of the Faith, in the Old Roman form
(*credo in sanctam ecclesiam*).   That it is the hand of Marcion
we do not doubt, not only because we have Tertullian directly
in evidence on the subject, but also because there is no passage
in the Epistles that would be more satisfactory to his anti-
Judaic mind.   There can be little doubt that the verses in
Galatians were stock quotations with Marcion and his followers.
We find also that the passage affirming the true Mother and

---

[1] For a similar instance take Acts vii. 17 where the original Greek appears
to have been

τῆς ἐπαγγελίας ἧς ὡμολόγησεν

for which the Bezan Latin is

promissionis quam pollicitus est,

and the Bezan Greek shows the alternative reading ἐπηγγείλατο

real Jerusalem to be the Church became one of the watchwords of the Paulician heresy which derives so much from Marcion. When the question came up amongst them as to the degree of honour to be given to the Mother of God, they used to say, " the true Theotokos is the heavenly Jerusalem, the Mother of believers."

But while we do not doubt that we have here the hand of Marcion, we hardly expected to find biblical evidence from before the middle of the second century for the currency of one of the Articles of the Old Roman Symbol, in the form which preceded the conventional ' holy catholic church [1].'

While we are drawing attention to the newly-published commentary and to its Marcionite reading it may be worth while to examine whether in a consecutive commentary on the Epistles, which shows Marcionite influence, we find any sugges- tions of the same arrangement of the Epistles as was found in Marcion's Apostolicon. If we may judge from Tertullian, the epistles stood in the order

Galatians, 1 and 2 Corinthians, Romans, 1 and 2 Thess., Ephes., Col., Phil., Philem.

The Armenian Commentary is arranged according to the current usage, which Zahn calls the Alexandrian usage, but there are suspicious traces of its having been re-arranged by the Armenian translator. In the opening of the epistle to the Romans, Ephrem adds to the text " that I may impart unto you some spiritual grace " the words " as I have done to your

---

[1] The natural suggestion was made by Zahn (l. c. col. 465) that the text of the Epistles upon which Ephrem is commenting was, like that of the Gospel, a text which had passed through Tatian's own hands, and which may have been brought back by him from Rome to Edessa, and have furnished the text from which the first Syriac version of the Pauline Epistles was made. " Wenn Marcion um 145 in Rom einen catholischen Text der Paulusbriefe in der Hand gehabt hat, welcher in sehr auffälligen Punkten mit dem ältesten erreichbaren syrischen Text zusammentrifft, so weiss ich dafür keine andere annehmbare Erklärung, als dass der erste syrische Uebersetzer der Paulusbriefe eine im Abendland geschriebene Handschrift seiner Arbeit zu Grunde gelegt hat. Am einfachsten bleibt die Annahme, dass der von Rom nach Mesopotamien heimgekehrte Tatian seinen Landsleuten den ersten ' Apostolos ' wie das erste ' Evangelium ' in ihrer Sprache gegeben hat."

fellows the Galatians and Corinthians." The suggestion is that
the commentator, who frequently poses as Paul, observes the
order, Galatians, Corinthians, Romans, and the suspicion is
confirmed when we find at the beginning of the epistle to the
Hebrews the words :

"Cum nec in epistolis scriptis ad Galatos, nec Corinthios, et
ad proximos quos viderat, id fecerit, neque in epistolis ad
Romanos datis, et ad caeteros quos non viderat, tale quoddam
egerit."

We may fairly conclude that the Epistles, at all events the
first ones, stood in the order which they occupied in Marcion's
Apostolicon. But Zahn points out that in the preface to
Philippians, Ephrem intimates that Colossians is to follow,
whereas in Marcion's order, Colossians preceded. I cannot,
however, in view of what has been noted as to the priority of
Galatians, believe he is right in saying that the order of the
Epistles in the Armenian text is certainly that of Ephrem.

Leaving now on one side the demonstration which Zahn
makes of the thoroughly Western character of the text of the
Epistles commented on by Ephrem, we pass on to the question
which we proposed to examine : viz. the existence or non-
existence of an Old Syriac text of the Acts. Are there any
traces of such a text in the Commentary on the Epistles ?

We must premise that in dealing with a question of this
kind which has to be resolved by the study of an Armenian
translation, we shall never be safe in concluding from the
existence of certain readings in the Armenian text to their
existence in the lost Syriac original unless the text vary from
the popular Armenian ; for the simple reason that the
translator accommodates his translation sometimes consciously
and sometimes unconsciously to the Armenian Vulgate, which
has undergone revision from the Latin. We need, therefore, to
be very careful with our steps in those cases where the
Armenian book before us agrees with the Armenian Vulgate.
Let us, then, ask the question whether Ephrem in this
recovered commentary makes any quotations from the Acts of
the Apostles, and what sort of text is involved in the Syriac

of such quotations.   We will begin by taking a passage from
2 Tim. iii. 11, where S. Paul reminds Timothy of the persecutions which happened to him in Antioch, Iconium, Lystra.
Ephrem begins by explaining that it is Antioch of Phrygia, not
Antioch of Syria that is meant: Antiochia autem non ista
Syriae, sed illa Phrygiae ; ubi excitarunt Judaei rectores
civitatis, et mulieres divites, et fecerunt tribulationem magnam
super eos, expulsis eis extra fines suos.

For this account we turn to Acts xiii. 50, where the text is

οἱ δὲ Ἰουδαῖοι παρώτρυναν τὰς σεβομένας γυναῖκας τὰς εὐσχήμονας καὶ τοὺς πρώτους τῆς πόλεως, καὶ ἐπήγειραν διωγμὸν
ἐπὶ τὸν Παῦλον καὶ Βαρνάβαν καὶ ἐξέβαλον αὐτοὺς ἀπὸ τῶν
ὁρίων αὐτῶν.

Ephrem's text agrees with the Peshito in translating
εὐσχήμονας by divites; but the expression 'fecerunt tribulationem' appears in the Bezan version of the passage which has

θλείψειν μεγάλην καὶ διωγμόν.

Ephrem goes on to tell us that "Iconii autem post
anteriorem tribulationem suscitarunt persecutionem, Judaei et
Gentiles, et lapidantes eum ac Barnabam, ejecerunt illos a
civitate."

The common text of the Acts knows nothing of two persecutions at Iconium, nor of any actual stoning of Paul and Barnabas, yet something like a previous persecution is implied in the
common text of Acts xiv. 2, where 'the Jews that were dis-
obedient stirred up and evilly affected the minds of the Gentiles
against the brethren.'   Neither does the account say that Paul
and Barnabas were expelled from the city.

When we turn to the Bezan text, we find first of all that
two distinct Iconian persecutions are given, the first being con-
cluded by the intimation that 'the Lord promptly gave peace';
the second stage of the persecution does not shew any actual
stoning on the part of the Iconians, at least not in the Greek
text, but when we turn to the Latin, which so often is superior
to the Greek in archaism, we find

> ut autem factum est impetus gentilium
> et iudaeorum cum magistribus ipsorum
> et iniuriauerunt et lapidauerunt eos

It may, of course, be said that the last line is simply a transcriptional error for

> ut iniuriarent et lapidarent;

but we notice that it is in agreement with the text of Ephrem, and suspect the Bezan Latin to be more archaic than its Greek. (Cf. also the Laudian Latin: *et contumeliis adficerunt eos et lapidarent* (*sic*).)

In 1 Cor. xiv. 23 (p. 77) Ephrem says " de Apostolis dixerunt eos musto plenos inebriatos esse "; the combination of the two passages involved is perfectly natural, but there is reason for believing it to have been in the Old Syriac, since a slightly different form of the combination is in the Peshito (of Acts ii. 13), which reads " They have drunk new wine and are intoxicated."

A more striking case will be Ephesians iv. 10 (p. 150), where the writer has not only quoted the text of the Acts, but incorporated two of the famous Western glosses (cf. Acts i. 5 in Cod. Bezae):

> ' Qui descendit, ipse est et qui ascendit super omnes caelos, id est, super omnes altitudines caelorum; ut impleret omnia quae dixit; istud est, quod dixerat; *quam recipitis vos* non post multos dies, *sed usque ad Pentecosten.*'

The addition of these glosses can hardly be due to a later hand than Ephrem; moreover there is no sign of them in the text of the Acts in the Peshito nor in the Armenian Vulgate; they are among the glosses for which no Syriac evidence has as yet been forthcoming; in fact their whole attestation, outside the Codex Bezae, seems to consist of certain passages of Augustine and of the Sahidic version.

The occurrence of this famous gloss from Acts i. 5 in the text of Ephrem must be considered very significant: moreover, the conjunction (*sed*) by which the gloss is connected with the text is important; the clause occupies the same place in

Ephrem's text as it does in the Codex Bezae, and it looks as if the motive for the gloss had been in the peculiar Greek order

$$ο\dot{υ} \ μετὰ \ πολλὰς \ ταύτας \ ἡμέρας,$$

instead of $μετ'$ $ο\dot{υ}$ $πολλὰς$ $ταύτας$ $ἡμέρας.$

Whether its origin be in a Greek antithesis or in a translator's expansion or the remark of a commentator, we will not discuss further at present. What we are occupied with is the existence of Western elements in the Syriac used by Ephrem.

Enough has been said to demonstrate this from the Commentary of Ephrem on the Pauline Epistles. Mr Chase's hypothesis of the existence of an Old Syriac text of the Acts is therefore a good one whatever may be the origin of the text. We will now pass on to prove it still more conclusively and in another way.

It would naturally suggest itself to any one who was in search of the Old Syriac of the Acts, to examine the commentaries on the Acts made by the Old Syrian fathers. The question then arises, Did Ephrem write any connected commentary on the Acts? If so, why should we spend our time in hunting out stray references to the Acts in commentaries on other books?

Unfortunately, though there is reason to believe that Ephrem wrote a commentary on the Acts of the Apostles, there are no traces of it in his published works, as far as I know; there remains, then, the possibility that fragments of it may be preserved in Greek or Syriac Catenae. As far as I have been able to make a search, no Syriac catena on the Acts has come to light; but happily for our investigation, the Armenians at Venice have published for us[1] a complete Catena on the Acts which is either a translation from the Syriac, or was made from materials existing in Armenian, which were derived from the Syriac by translation, and this Catena contains a large number of extracts from Ephrem. The greater part of the book is, however, taken from the writings of Chrysostom. If we assume that the Catena was made, as seems likely, late in the eleventh century, it is probable

---

[1] *Comm. on Act. Apost.* Venice, 1839.

that it was made up out of works existing in Armenian; in that case it is not unreasonable to hope that the complete text may some day be recovered in Armenian. But whatever may have been the manner of its composition we shall be able (by the kind help of my good friend Mr Conybeare who has responded to my appeal for a translation) to extract a good deal of Ephrem from its pages, and to come to a decided opinion as to the ·nature of the text upon which Ephrem worked.

The first thing that will be noticed is that the compiler of the Catena is largely under the influence of the Armenian Vulgate, so that we shall have to be careful in our interpretations on account of the difficulty of discriminating between the sources of the Armenian text. We will, therefore, bracket the texts from the Catena where they agree closely with the Vulgate.

The Catena is divided into chapters, and the initial excerpt of each chapter is left unascribed; perhaps the scribe meant to illuminate the first names and afterwards omitted to do so; these sections had better be laid on one side. They are very likely Chrysostom's in view of the preponderance of extracts from that writer.

We shall first discuss some of the more striking sections from the lost Commentary, and then we will subjoin the text of the major part of the Ephrem fragments as an Appendix.

We will first draw attention to the account of Paul's visit to Philippi, which is, as is well known, much expanded in the Bezan text, and often with great appearance of originality.

The commentary on Acts xvi. 35 begins as follows (from Ephrem ?):

p. 300. "Perhaps the heads of the army knew all the great wonders which had occurred; and so they did not venture of themselves to release them, but sent to the gaoler to dismiss them, as it were, by stealth.

p. 301 (Ephr.). The Astaritai were afraid and full of fear, they the mighty of the city, of the earthquake, and knew truly that this earthquake happened on account of them, but they did not undertake to avow it. They sent secretly to bring them out."

Here it seems clear that the text before Ephrem must have contained a statement very like that in Codex Bezae:

CYNHΛΘON OIC CTPATHΓOI
EΠI TO AYTO EIC THN AΓOPAN
KAI ANAMNHCΘENTEC
TON CEICMON TON ΓEΓONOTA EΦOBHΘHCAN.

(Astaritai is probably a misreading of a transliterated Syriac ܐܣܛܪ̈ܛܝܘ; in fact the word is so transferred in the Peshito.)

The Commentary then proceeds with vv. 35—37 as in the Armenian Vulgate; then follows (p. 302)

c. xvi. 39 (Ephr.). "So then that this favour might be unto them, they came and besought of them, saying, We knew not that ye were just, even as the earthquake indeed presaged about you. So then we ask of you this favour, depart from this city, lest the same men gather together after the earthquake against you, (the same) who before the earthquake were gathered together."

Cf. with this the verse as current in the Codex Bezae:

EΦOBHΘHCAN KAI ΠAPAΓENOMENOI
META ΦIΛΩN ΠOΛΛΩN EIC THN ΦYΛAKHN
ΠAPEKAΛECAN AYTOYC EZEΛΘEIN EIΠONTEC
HΓNOHCAMEN TA KAΘ YMAC
OTI ECTAI ANΔPEC ΔIKAIOI
KAI EZAΓAΓONTEC
ΠAPEKAΛECAN AYTOYC ΛEΓONTEC
EK THC ΠOΛEΩC TAYTHC EZEΛΘATE
MHΠOTE ΠAΛIN CYNCTPAΦΩCIN HMEIN
EΠIKPAZONTEC KAΘ YMΩN.

It is clear that some text very like that of Codex Bezae must have been before Ephrem.

Turn in the next place to c. xvii. 15 (p. 310):

(Ephr.) "So he came as far as the shore, receding. But the Holy Spirit prevented him from preaching lest they should slay him. [And those who conducted Paul, led him as far as

Athens and having received] from Paul [a command to Silas and Timotheus that they should at once come to him] at Athens. [And they went] to him when they received the command."

The Bezan text with which we may make comparison is as follows (the chief expansions being bracketed):

ΤΟΝ ΜΕΝ ΟΥΝ ΠΑΥΛΟΝ

ΟΙ ΑΔΕΛΦΟΙ ΕΞΑΠΕCΤΕΙΛΑΝ

ΑΠΕΛΘΕΙΝ ΕΠΙ ΤΗΝ ΘΑΛΑCCΑΝ

ΥΠΕΜΕΙΝΕΝ ΔΕ Ο CΕΙΛΑC ΚΑΙ Ο ΤΙΜΟΘΕΟC ΕΚΕΙ

ΟΙ ΔΕ ΚΑΤΑCΤΑΝΟΝΤΕC ΤΟΝ ΠΑΥΛΟΝ

ΗΓΑΓΟΝ ΕΩC ΑΘΗΝΩΝ

[ΠΑΡΗΛΘΕΝ ΔΕ ΤΗΝ ΘΕCCΑΛΙΑΝ

ΕΚΩΛΥΘΗ ΓΑΡ ΕΙC ΑΥΤΟΥC

ΚΗΡΥΞΑΙ ΤΟΝ ΛΟΓΟΝ]

ΛΑΒΟΝΤΕC ΔΕ ΕΝΤΟΛΗΝ [ΠΑΡΑ ΠΑΥΛΟΥ]

ΠΡΟC ΤΟΝ CΕΙΛΑΝ ΚΑΙ ΤΙΜΟΘΕΟΝ

ΟΠΩC ΕΝ ΤΑΧΕΙ ΕΛΘΩCΙΝ

ΠΡΟC ΑΥΤΟΝ ΕΞΗΕCΑΝ.

It is clear, then, that Ephrem had before him an expanded text like that of D; the statement that Paul was prevented by the Holy Spirit from preaching in Thessaly must have been in his copy. One of the smaller glosses in the Codex Bezae was also present (παρα παυλου) and perhaps the words εἰς τὰς Ἀθήνας were also in the text. The peculiar expression of Ephrem that 'Paul came to the sea, receding,' is obscure. The words mean literally 'giving way' (? = ἀναχωρῶν). It is curious that the Latin of Cod. Bezae has

abire ad mare uersus

where *ad mare uersus* is perfectly good Latin[1].

Is it possible that this *versus* has been understood as *conversus* or *reversus*? Whatever be the origin of the statement there can be no doubt that Ephrem had a Bezan text.

---

[1] Cp. Caesar, *B. G.* vi. 33, Labienum ad Oceanum versus in illas partes proficisci iubet.

One more proof shall be given : from Acts xix. 38, 39,
p. 352 [Ephr. ?], "This Demetrius, vile and shameless, he says,
he and the children (παῖδες) of his craft, if they have any suit
with one another, let them stand forward and make it clear to
the hegemon. And [if there be] any other [enquiry let] it be
[pronounced on in the lawful assembly].

We compare as before

ΕΙ ΜΕΝ ΟΥΝ ΔΗΜΗΤΡΙΟC [ΟΥΤΟC]
ΟΙ ΚΑΙ CΥΝ ΑΥΤΩ ΤΕΧΝΕΙΤΕ
ΕΧΟΥCΙ ΠΡΟC [ΑΥΤΟΥC] ΤΙΝΑ ΛΟΓΟΝ
ΑΓΟΡΑΙΟΙ ΑΓΟΝΤΑΙ ΚΑΙ ΑΝΘΥΠΑΤΟΙ ΕΙCΙΝ
ΕΝΚΑΛΙΤΩCΑΝ ΑΛΛΗΛΟΙC
ΕΙ ΔΕ ΠΕΡΙ ΕΤΕΡΩΝ ΕΠΙΖΗΤΕΙΤΕ
ΕΝ ΤΩ ΝΟΜΩ ΕΚΚΛΗCΙΑ ΕΠΙΛΥΘΗCΕΤΑΙ.

Here Ephrem has the added οὗτος of the Bezan text ; he
has also the added αὐτοὺς which has been understood as
ἑαυτοὺς, as if Demetrius and his fellows might have quarrels
inter se ; further he has read περαιτέρω (which surely must
be original) as περι ετερων which we find in D. (This variant
is therefore a primitive Greek error on the part of a copyist.)
It is clear, therefore, and instances might be abundantly
multiplied, that Ephrem's text was in the later chapters of
the Acts closely connected with that of the Codex Bezae[1].

Another passage in the commentary on the Pauline Epistles
which invites study, but from which it is not easy to draw very
definite conclusions, is 1 Cor. ii. 8, where Ephrem remarks :

Id est, quod apostoli dixerunt, "Scimus, quia per errorem
deceptionis haec fecistis; convertimini igitur, et poenitemini,
et nemo id vobis reputabit ad peccatum."

---

[1] The last extract seems to be acephalous, but it evidently belongs to the
same fabric as the others. The Peshito helps us to restore the original Syriac

ܘܐܘܢܓܠܝܘܢ ܘܩܕܝܫܘܗܝ ܗܢܐ ܡܢ ܐ

It looks as if οὗτος were due to a wrong line-division ; we should read

ΕΙ ΜΕΝ ΟΥΝ ΔΗΜΗΤΡΙΟC
ΟΥΤΟC ΚΑΙ ΟΙ CΥΝ ΑΥΤΩ ΤΕΧΝΕΙΤΑΙ

The reference is to Acts iii. 17: and although it is not quite easy to detach the text of the passage from its setting, there seems to be no reason to doubt that the text of Ephrem had the Western reading which appears in Cod. Bezae as ἐπιστάμεθα (d² = *scimus*) and instead of οἶδα (where Irenaeus has *scio*).

The origin of the variant appears to be Greek, and to be an attempt to avoid the confusion caused by the presence in the text of μὲν after οἶδα, which might be read as οἶδα μὲν or as οἴδαμεν. The existence of this μὲν is evidenced by the double fact that Cod. Bezae has carried it into the next line (ὑμεῖς μὲν), and instead of οἴδαμεν has the equivalent ἐπιστάμεθα.

We notice also that the text used by Ephrem did not contain the expansion at the end of the expression

$$\kappa\alpha\tau\grave{\alpha}\ \mathring{\alpha}\gamma\nu o\iota\alpha\nu\ \mathring{\epsilon}\pi\rho\acute{\alpha}\xi\alpha\tau\epsilon\ [\pi o\nu\eta\rho\acute{o}\nu],$$

which is found in the Codex Bezae, in Irenaeus and elsewhere, but some simpler expansion, probably the same as occurs in the Peshito, 'ye did this (ܗܢܐ).'

The rest of the verse as quoted by Ephrem is obscure and paraphrastic, and may be from his own hand. On the whole the text seems to be Western in character, but not as decidedly as we should have expected.

Acts xx. 29 is also quoted by Ephrem in the introduction to the apocryphal 3rd Epistle to the Corinthians, but apparently in the terms of the Peshito[1].

Probably we should also notice the commentary of Ephrem on Rom. viii. 7 (p. 26), in which he contrasts the imperfection of the law with the fulness of the Gospel: he says that Christians really do obey the law,

"etsi circumcisi, ac sabbati observatores, existiment nos adversarios esse legis, eo quod superflua illa legis soluta sunt desuper. Si autem illa occidisset atque salvasset, oportuisset

---

[1] But observe that 'ut convertant auditores ad sequendos se' where the Greek text is τοῦ ἀποσπᾶν is in agreement with Irenaeus 'ut convertant' and Cod. Bezae τοῦ ἀποστρέφειν as well as with the Peshito

ܐܝܟ ܕܢܗܦܟܘܢ ܠܬܠܡܝܕܐ ܕܢܐܙܠܘܢ ܒܬܪܗܘܢ

We have also an allusion to the story of Elymas on p. 247, but without any Old Syriac traces, as far as I see.

eam prius in cordibus inscriptam fuisse. Tu autem vide, quia
neque justitia plena est illa, neque in ea est illa justitia, quae
dicit, Quod tibi malum videtur, proximo ne facias."

The argument is that circumcision is a superfluous part of
the law which has been abolished. If it had been a part of the
true law which kills and makes alive, it would have had to be
heart-circumcision. But the old imperfect statement of the
law did not contain the precept to do nothing to the neighbour
which we should ourselves dislike.

It seems not unreasonable to enquire whether Ephrem in
his text of Acts xv. (vv. 20 and 29) may not have had the
addition of the famous negative precept to the Jerusalem
Concordat. This is an important and interesting question,
inasmuch as the reading is perhaps the oldest reading extant
of those which are called Western. It has been pointed out by
Seeberg[1] that the interpolation in Acts xv. 29 must have been
in the text of the Acts used by Aristides the Apologist: for
Aristides tells us in his summary of the early Christian ethics,
that "they do not worship idols in the form of man; and whatever they do not wish that others should do to them, they do
not practise towards any one; and they do not eat of the meats
of idol sacrifices, for they are undefiled." The apparent want of
sequence in the precepts is explained at once by a reference to
the interpolated passage in the Acts in which the negative
Golden Rule is made a pendent to the regulations against
eating idol-meats, &c. Accordingly Seeberg says, and I do
not see that exception can be taken to his reasoning (except by
denying the genuineness of the Syriac text) that

"Hieraus folgt deutlich, dass Aristides den Spruch nicht in
der Form der Didache, sondern in der in das N. T. übergegan-
genen Form gekannt hat. Da er nun den Spruch mit der
Enthaltung von den εἰδωλόθυτα zusammen anfürt, so kann
nicht bezweifelt werden, dass er in seinem Text der Apostel-
geschichten diesen Spruch, wie Irenäus, bereits gelesen hat.
Dann ist Aristides der älteste Zeuge für diese Interpolation......
Bald darauf folgt übrigens bei Aristides die Enthaltung von der

[1] *Die Apologie des Aristides*, p. 213.

συνουσία ἄνομος (cf. die πορνεία der Apgesch.). Diese Stelle erweist also sowol die kirchliche Benützung der Apgesch. zur Zeit des Aristides als das Vorhandensein der Interpolation in der Mitte des 2. Jarh."

The genuineness of the Syriac text appears further to be established by the consideration that no reason can be assigned for the insertion of the precept by a translation at a point where its connexion with the context is not at first sight obvious, as well as by the reflection that the passage, if genuine, would be out of date and almost unintelligible to a literary pirate in the seventh century[1].

Whatever, then, be the date of the first appearance of the variant in the text of the Acts, we are sure that it was extant very early, and need not be surprised if we should find it current in the text commented on by Ephrem. We do not, however, wish to speak too positively as to the source of the quotation in Ephrem: and that for various reasons: the negative precept turns up everywhere in the early Church, having been absorbed, in the first instance, from Jewish ethics. Moreover it seems likely that it was not only interpolated into the Acts, but, if we may judge from certain remarks of Tertullian against Marcion, it also was current in Marcionized copies of the Gospel of Luke. Further the form in which

---

[1] Mr Chase, I observe, quotes the incorrect Greek of the Apology, and so avoids the conclusions of the foregoing argument; and explains the occurrence of the negative precept in Aristides as a case of apologetic absorption from the text of some form of the Διδαχή. But even in the incorrect text, the connexion between Aristides and the interpolated Acts is so close that he is forced to admit that "from such an apologetic passage the saying naturally passed into a similar context in Acts xv." [This is dangerously near to the admission of a Greek original for the gloss. Did the Apologists write in Syriac?] He then makes a laboured and obscure argument to prove that after the passage had been absorbed into the text of the Acts from Aristides or some similar Apologist, it passed into the text of Theophilus of Antioch from the text of the Acts through the medium of a Syriac version (cp. Theoph. ad Autol. II. 34). The difference in the treatment of the two cases is, we may conjecture, due to the fact that Mr Chase wishes to go to Antioch for the origin of his textual corruptions; and does not wish to go to Athens! He deals in a somewhat similar manner with the Western text of the Acts which is quoted in Polycarp's Epistle to the Philippians: if it had only been Ignatius! (Cf. Chase, p. 21 on Acts ii. 24.)

Ephrem quotes is not the exact form in the Acts; he uses the expression "quod tibi malum videtur" which is much nearer to the Talmudic form of the precept : and the same peculiarity appears where Ephrem quotes the precept in Romans iii. 21; where it is expressly called, in opposition to the statement previously quoted[1], a precept of the *law* (aut ipsam legem docere mansuetudinem et fidem; ut exempli gratia quum dicit : *quod tibi malum videtur ne aliis feceris*) : we should not then feel justified in employing the passage quoted from Rom. viii. as a proof that Ephrem had the famous interpolation in his copy of the Acts.

From two separate lines of enquiry, therefore, we have discussed the question of the existence of an Old Syriac text of the Acts, and have removed Mr Chase's hypothesis into the region of fact. Setting on one side the question as to what the result of this discovery will be upon the criticism of the text, and it cannot fail to be far-reaching, we can only most cordially congratulate Mr Chase on the complete and thorough verification of the assumption with which he commences his investigation into the peculiarities of the Western text. It is not often that a speculation is so rapidly justified from unexpected quarters[2]. It remains to be seen whether the reason-

---

[1] Ephrem is no model of consistent interpretation; he loves alternatives : the ἄλλως whose equivalent is employed so often in his works is his own, and not the suggestion of a later hand.

[2] Of course I am aware that Mr Chase desiderates in the working out of his theory, not merely one old Syriac text, but many : in one single passage he requires sometimes as many as three separate versions! He justifies this view of the variety of the primitive Syriac texts by quoting the following remarks of Dr Hort with regard to the Curetonian text of the Gospels. "The rapid variation which we know the Greek and Latin texts to have undergone in the earlier centuries could hardly be absent in Syria; so that a single MS. cannot be expected to tell us more of the Old Syriac generally than we could learn from any one average Old Latin MS. respecting Old Latin texts generally." Mr Chase does not notice that when he has assigned the Syriac version as the *cause* of the Greek and Latin Western Variants, these remarks of Dr Hort no longer apply. The comparison in that case between the progressive changes of the Syriac and those of the Graeco-Latin texts must be made between the Syriac version and the Western texts *considered as unaffected by the Syriac version*, if any analogy between the two sets of phenomena is to hold good. But on Mr Chase's theory the variation of Graeco-Latin texts is almost *nil* when the Syriac reactions are removed.

ing which he has based upon the hypothesis can also be justified.

We will now add as an appendix the more important of the extracts which we have been able to collect of the commentary of Ephrem on the Acts.

APPENDIX.

EXTRACTS FROM THE ARMENIAN VERSION OF EPHREM'S COMMENTARY ON THE ACTS. Translated by F. C. CONYBEARE, with some additional notes.

p. 13 (Ephrem). The author of the Acts of the Apostles was Luke the Evangelist. He was not indeed with Christ from the commencement of his preaching, but he attached himself to the apostles of Christ from the very first descent of the Spirit and before. And although his gospel was only written by him according as he heard from the apostles of Christ, yet of the Acts of the Apostles which he wrote he was himself an eye-witness. He wrote his Gospel, because he saw that certain impostors had written out of their heads a gospel under the name of "the infancy of Christ our Lord," and other books of questions (*hartzouadzots*, but ? read *herdzouadzots* = of heresies) under the name of Mary and of the disciples of Christ, in which they say that after the resurrection that first-born one ascended after 18 months; whereas the disciples write about him that he after the fortieth day exactly ascended into heaven. Luke then in order to hinder the false books of heterodox writers by (? or from) the gospel of our Lord Jesus Christ, who concoct about the Lord Jesus an old age and a youth of works (narrating some things before his baptism and others after his ascension on the fortieth day)—therefore he sets in his book of the Acts of the Apostles a beginning and an end of the works of our Lord, in imitation of the other Evangelists, beginning from the baptism of the Lord by John, and continuing to his ascension on the 40th day: in order to shew that every work whatever ascribed to Christ earlier than his baptism and subsequent to his ascension after 40 days, is a work alien to Christ our Lord. And it is clear from the fact that Christ himself said to his disciples, "If I go not, the Comforter will not come." And the Comforter came on the completion of Pentecost, the 50th day after his resurrection. It is, therefore, manifest that on the completion of the 40 days' term, as the Apostles say, Jesus ascended. And those impostors are false who say he ascended after 18 months. So Luke wrote about the resurrection of our Lord. about his Ascension and the Coming of the Spirit and the increase of the disciples and about all that followed[1].

p. 19. Acts i. 2 (Ephrem). [Until the day of commanding the Apostles by the Holy Spirit.] As I said above, at the beginning of the Acts of the Lord he also sets a term, saying ' until the day of commanding,' which is the day of his ascent, —in order to silence the liars.

p. 20 (Ephrem). Now he shewed that he remained after the Cross not without miracles ($\sigma\eta\mu\epsilon\hat{\imath}a$), but in many miracles ($\sigma\eta\mu\epsilon\hat{\imath}a$) and many signs ($\tau\epsilon\kappa\mu\eta\rho\iota a$) which he wrought in the forty days: as he appeared to them in all likenesses, now known and now unknown: according as in another place it saith: "Their eyes were holden that they should not know him," and "He was made known to them."

p. 21. Acts i. 4 (Ephrem). Not as having any natural wants, therefore, of food, but making a concession in order to a convincing demonstration of the resurrection.

p. 22 (Ephrem[2]). And because they were frightened, first he led them forth into Galilee, that without suspicion they might hear what was said. And when they heard, lo! for forty days he tarried with them, and commanded them not to leave Jerusalem nor to go forth to preach before receiving the Spirit. As no one allows soldiers to engage in battle before being armed, so he did not allow them to enter the affray and conquer (? be conquered) before the Coming of the Spirit.

---

[1] For the doctrine of an Ascension after 18 months see Irenaeus (ed. Mass. p. 14) where the belief is given as a peculiarity of the Valentinians. "καὶ τοὺς λοιποὺς δεκαοκτὼ Αἰῶνας φανεροῦσθαι, διὰ τοῦ μετὰ τὴν ἐκ νεκρῶν ἀνάστασιν δεκαοκτὼ μησὶ λέγειν διατετριφέναι αὐτὸν σὺν τοῖς μαθηταῖς." See also Ascensio Isaiae (ed. Dillmann, c. ix. p. 43).

[2] Almost all of this section will be found in Chrysostom in loc. (ed. Savile, p. 611).

And again because of the many who were about to believe in
Jerusalem, he made it necessary for them to abide there;
and again that the Jews might not say that they left alone
those whom they knew and went forth to strangers, because of
their hatred or of glory, and lest being attacked they might
run away from them, even for sake of the very crucifiers they
give out the tidings of the resurrection in that city, where
the unjust slaying of Christ by them took place, in order that
the outer heathen might easily believe, seeing the slayers of
Christ come to believe in Him, and the crucifiers become
preachers of his resurrection.

But that the disciples might not say: 'how shall we
remain among the cruel slayers?' nor flee after his removal he
dissolves their suspicion by the promise of the Spirit; to
first bestow it on them there. For by this hope as with a
chain, he will detain them in Jerusalem, sitting and awaiting
there the promise of the good news of the Father, who by the
prophets saith 'I will pour out of my spirit upon all flesh.'

p. 24. Acts i. 5 (Ephrem, Chrysostom, *sic !*). And not
only doth he avow himself to be great beyond comparison, but
* he shews his disciples to be greater than John, saying, Ye shall
be baptised (? baptise), for they were destined to baptise even
others in the Holy Spirit. And he did not say, I baptise you,
but, Ye shall be baptised, teaching us to be humble. But that
he himself it was that baptised them by the Spirit, is clear
from the testimony of John; for he said; "He shall baptise
you with the Holy Spirit and with fire."*

And that they received the Spirit in the upper-chamber is
clear. * But how saith he, 'ye shall be baptised,' there being
no water in the upper-chamber? I answer that the Spirit is
supreme, by which the water also energises ($\dot{\epsilon}\nu\epsilon\rho\gamma\epsilon\hat{\imath}$). In like
manner he himself is called anointed, not with sensible oil
indeed, but with the Spirit of joy. And in another fashion
(we may explain it): they had long before been baptised with
water by John: for if publicans were baptised, much more they,

---

* The words between asterisks are from Chrysostom as may be seen by reference to his published Commentary. The double heading is therefore doubtful.

whose destiny it was to be baptised and to baptise with the Holy Spirit. For though in our time it is possible to be baptised at once with water and Spirit, it was then in the time of the disciples (only possible) in separate times.*

p. 28 (c. i. 7) (Ephr.). And this with so much firmness, because he willed not to reveal to them these days of his ascending, which they saw with their own eyes.

p. 30 (c. i. 8) (Ephr.). [For ye shall receive power] and courage at the coming of the Spirit on you. And ye shall go out from the upper-room, and shall be manifest to the world, witnesses of my resurrection and of what ye heard and saw from me not only in Jerusalem, city of crucifiers, where indeed ye are afraid, but also among the Samaritans, and all races.

p. 31 (c. i. 10) (Ephr.). [And the cloud] hid (or covered) [him from their eyes.]

p. 34 (c. i. 12) (acephalous but probably Ephrem).

Then [they returned to Jerusalem from the mountain called of Olives...which is near to Jerusalem according to a Sabbath's journey].

(c. i. 13). [And when they entered] Jerusalem, as they received a command not to leave Jerusalem, [they went into the upper-room, where the lodgings of course were, etc.]... But Simeon (Shmawon) the Zealot is by Matthew and Mark called Simon the Cananaean. Perhaps in the Hebrew tongue he is called Zealot. And it is averred by many that he is son of Joseph father of the Lord, and brother of the Lord. Moreover Judas (brother) of Jacob, was brother of the same Simon and son of Joseph, who also was brother of the Lord. This one wrote the Catholic epistle which in his name is called the epistle of Judas, in which at the beginning out of humility instead of calling himself brother of the Lord, he writes brother of Jacob. And hence it is clear that he is the same whom Matthew and Mark call Lebaeus and Thadaeus, so that they and Luke do not respectively name different persons, but only one and the same person by different names And no wonder if in Hebrew there was a plenty of double names and multiple names, whence the ambiguity in question of the Evangelists as to Thadaeus and Judas is one of name only, not of persons. For of the first set

chosen by Christ not one perished, but only Judas the traitor.
It is certain then that the other Thadaeus who was with
Abgar was of the Seventy, to which fact their tombs also
testify. For Thadaeus, one of the Seventy, died in Armenia in
the region Artazon; but Judas of Jacob who in Matthew and
Mark is Thadaeus, one of the Twelve, died in Ormi in Armenia. Thus the agreement of the Evangelists as to the names
of the Apostles is confirmed.

p. 38 (c. i. 17) (Ephr.). [because he was in our number along
with us .... and there had fallen to him the lot of this service.]

p. 42 (c. i. 25) (Ephr.). [From which passed away Judas to
go to his own place]...not to that which is full of light, which
the Lord promised him, but into darkness.

p. 45 (c. ii. 2) (Ephr.). A violent sound of a wind came
about in the house where were gathered together the disciples
of Jesus and a sweet smell was wafted from the violence of
the wind and filled all the house[1].

p. 45 (c. ii. 2) (Nyss. Ephr.). [And filled all the house in
which they were sitting.] And how did the wind fill the
house? Manifestly with a sweet smell and with a bright
light.

p. 47 (c. ii. 3) (Ephr.). [And it sat upon each of them.]
That is to say, the tongues appeared and sat upon one by one
of them. It is clear that they severally (ἔκασται) sat on each,
the whole of the parts sitting on one by one of them. For
which reason and because of the sameness of the nature, he
gathers the whole of the parts into one, and says in the
singular: It sat upon each of them.

p. 49 (c. ii. 6) (Ephr.). [When there was this voice, there
came together the crowd and was confused.] The voice which
came from heaven was audible to all the citizens. And the
smell, which from the violence of the wind was wafted, gathered
and brought thither the many. This is the voice which there
was.

---

[1] Compare the following section and ii. 6, also ii. 32. We may suspect
that there was something in the text which provoked the comment about
the sweet smell. Was it an assimilation to Isaiah vi. 'The house was filled
with smoke,' viz. of incense?

p. 49 (c. ii. 6) (Ephr.). These then are those whom the terrible[1] voice moved to fear and the smell of fragrance brought and mustered together—when they saw the Galileans talking in all tongues, were amazed as he says : [For they heard them speak in their own tongues].

p 52 (c. ii. 14) (aceph.). [Ye men etc. . . . . not as ye think] that we are filled with new wine. [For it is but the third hour of the day.]

p. 55 (c. ii. 20) (Ephr.). For as the dawn is sign of the rising of the sun, so the signs on the day of the cross of Christ are prognostics of the pouring out of the Spirit of God

p. 56 (c. ii. 20) (Ephr.). Whose light was given to the heathen and the vapour of smoke for the exacting from them of the requital of the blood of Christ and of the just. And there is darkened upon them the sun before the taking of them into a lake of fire, of which he says, [Until there be come the day of the Lord great and famous].

p. 58 (c. ii. 22) (Ephr.). He proclaims him man, that as with milk he may feed them with the Gospel, and so that when they be perfected, they may proclaim him judge, creator and God.

p. 62 (c. ii. 32) (Ephr.). [To whom all we] are witnesses. And to us are witness the violent voice which breathed and the sweet smell which was wafted and the strange tongues which we speak.

p. 66 (c. ii. 38) (Ephr.). For the remission which is hidden in his baptism absolves you from lawlessness, for you crucified him. And when ye are absolved and pure, then ye become worthy of the gift of the Spirit which ye saw in us, ye also. And he confirms his argument and says [For to you is the good news and to your children] Manifest is that good tidings given by Joel, 'I will pour out of my spirit.'

p. 73 (c. iii. 1) (Ephr.). But some say, because he was inexperienced, and did not know how to walk, for he had never walked.

p. 94 (c. iv. 26, 27) (Ephr.). [Because of the Lord and his anointed.] Because in dishonouring Christ they dishonoured

---

[1] Probably a misreading of a Syriac text 'the voice of power.' Cp. p. 62,

the Father whom they did not dishonour (?). [For there were gathered indeed in this city against thy holy Son Jesus whom thou anointedst, Herod and Pontius Pilate with tribes and multitudes of Israel to do whatever thy hand and will aforetime determined to come to pass.]

p. 102 (c. v. 1) (Ephr.). Thus were slain the house of Ananias, not only because they thieved and hid, but because they feared not, wishing to trick those in whom the Holy Spirit that searches all was dwelling.

p. 115 (c. v. 37) (Ephr.). [After him, he says, arose Judas a Galilean in the days of there being a district-writing, and caused to revolt a great multitude after him.] Satan then raised them up before the birth and at the birth of our Lord. For he heard about his birth from the words of the angel who was with Zachariah and Mariam, and beheld that Simeon the old man was prevented, so as not to taste death till he should see our Lord Jesus Christ, and he was eager by this revolt to damage the plan of Christ. But through his haste as [he], so also this one [was destroyed] and those who [complied] with him [were scattered].

p. 127 (c. iv. 13) (Ephr.). But because they ridiculed the apostles as being simple and unlearned, he began to repeat to them the Scriptures, beginning from Abraham he summarises down to Christ and to their shamelessness.

p. 144 (c. vii. 43) (Ephr.). [Ye took, he says, the tent of Moloch] that is the cause of sacrifice, [and the star of your god Hrempha]...[the images which ye made to worship them]... For because thereof [I will transplant you to the other side of Babylon[1]]....But even [the tent of witness was with our fathers in the wilderness, as he commanded who spake with Moses, to make it according to the model which he saw]....He declares then that all this was so, and they had no temple. Nay more, there being the tent, there were no sacrifices. [Surely ye did not bring to me] victims [and offerings] he says. Mark how, although they had the tent of witness, it helped them nothing, nor the signs that were previous and subsequent. But all the

---

[1] It will be noticed that here the text [= Arm. Vulg.] is against that of Cod. D which for ἐπέκεινα Βαβυλῶνος has ἐπὶ τὰ μέρη B.

bones were destroyed and fell to the ground[1]. And he adds
[in the desert,...which our fathers received and bore] suc-
ceeding one another [along with Joshua] in the possession of the
Canaanites,...[whom] also [God drove out, from the face of our
fathers...Until the days of David], he says, there was no temple.
He [found grace before God and prayed to find a home for the
God of Jacob...Furthermore Solomon built to him a house.]
But not that the Highest dwells in temples made by hands...
[the heavens are my throne and the earth the footstool of my
feet...What sort of house will ye build me], he says, [or what
place of my repose? For all this did my hand make.]

p. 146 (c. vii. 51) (Ephr.). [O ye stiff-necked], he says, [and
uncircumcised in heart].

p. 152 (c. vii. 59) (Ephr.). [They stoned Stephen who was
crying aloud and saying: Lord Jesus, receive my spirit.]

p. 153 (c. viii. 1) (Ephr.). And it is similar that on this day
he took their goods as spoil; which things the apostle praises:
"Receive with joy the plundering of your goods[2]." And they all
were dispersed into the villages of Judaea and Samaria, except
the disciples[3].

p. 154 (c. viii. 3) (Ephr.). [But Saul was doing harm to the
Church. From house to house he went, dragged off men and
women, threw them into prison.]

p. 155 (c. viii. 5) (Ephr.). Philip then went down thither and
at the power of his signs he filled the land of Samaria with his
teaching, on such a scale that Simon Magus also, who startled
the Samaritans with his magic, undertook to come down with
the Samaritans for the washing of the font, as the Evangelist
relates in due order.

p. 158 (c. viii. 14) (Ephr.). And therefore they sent Peter and
John that by their laying on of hands the Samaritans may
receive the Spirit of signs and may astonish the children of
Jerusalem by the works of the Spirit which the Samaritans

---

[1] An allusion to 1 Kings xiii. 3; or is it the equivalent of 'whose carcases
fell in the wilderness'?

[2] Heb. x. 34.

[3] Here we should have looked for the Western gloss 'who remained in
Jerusalem.'

performed. [Then they laid hands on them and they received
the Holy Spirit.] It is clear that making prayer (as has been
said) they laid their hands. For the Holy Spirit was not
simply given nor could they give it. but there was need of much
asking. For it is not the same thing to get healing and to get
the power of healing. [Simon having seen that when the
Apostles laid on] hands [there was given the Holy Spirit, he
gave them money and said: Give also to me this power, that
on whomsoever I may lay hands, he may receive the Holy
Spirit]. Simon, he says, having seen. But perhaps he did not
see that no signs were manifested by the Samaritans...(p. 159)
he laid silver before them : why ?...wherefore Peter says to him :
[Thy silver be with thee unto destruction] for thou dost not use
it as it is right:...[because thou hast thought to obtain the gifts
of God by money] thinking little of the freedom of God's gifts...
[there is not for thee part and share in that matter...thy heart]
he says [is not right before God...Repent thou] he says [of
those evil] thoughts [of thine, and pray the Lord that there
may be remission to thee of the sinful thoughts of thy heart]...
he said that there may be remission to thee of the deceitful
thoughts of thy heart and from the bitter bonds of greed in
which thou art entrammelled...[For unto the bitterness of
wrath and unto the entanglement of unrighteousness I behold
thee]...the magician said [Do ye pray for me unto the Lord,
that there come not upon me aught of the things of which ye
have spoken[1]].

p. 163 (c. viii 27) (Ephr.). But it is likely that on this
account he came, for that he received it in succession from the
tradition of the queen of the South who came to worship in
the temple in the days of Solomon.

p. 166 (c viii. 40) (Ephr.). Wherefore as he went up out of
the font of baptism, there settled forthwith on him the Spirit of
the power of works. That by works of the Spirit which he
wrought in India, the cross which he preached might be faith-

---

[1] Here there do not seem to be any signs of the influence of the Western
text which we should expect, such as the addition of the word 'evil' in the
last line, or the account of Simon's ceaseless weeping.

fully reverenced[1]. And an angel of the Lord snatched up Philip and the Eunuch no longer saw him. But in the old copies of the translation he says: the Spirit of the Lord snatched up Philip[2]: and often he repeats 'the Spirit'; I think because he would make it clear that in the snatching up by the angel of Philip he became invisible to the Eunuch, lest the angel appearing in gross form, as to many in human shape, the Eunuch should think him to be a man.

p. 168 (c. ix. 2) (Ephr.). But he, as if no one sent him, himself with obstinate will, [having come to the High Priest, asked of him letters to Damascus to the synagogues; in order that if he find anyone of that way, men or women, he may bring them bound to Jerusalem.]

p. 169 (c. ix. 3) (Ephr.). With the light then he blinded him and so frightened him and with awful fear of his glory he extinguished his rage, and with gentle voice he mollified him, in which also he was persuaded to confide. And because he feared to contemn the humility of our Lord, who appeared to him with so gentle an utterance, and he was struck with fear of dishonouring his might, who by the mighty light startled him. And while he lay prone on the earth, dazed not after the voice but before the voice, lost in wonder as to who from heaven blinded him, for Jesus was not risen from the dead as he thought. But when he said to him in censure; [Saul, Saul, why persecutest thou me?] what wrong hast thou suffered from me that thou doest this to me? he fainted (?) in his mind, saying, I persecute, because of the Lord of heaven; and not, I persecute him who dwells in heaven. So he asked: Who art thou, Lord, who in thy heavens art persecuted? For I persecute Jesus who is among the dead, along with his disciples.

p. 171 (c. ix. 7) (Ephr.). But the strong illumination they saw not, lest they too be blinded and there be confusion. But he blinded Saul strictly, but pitied them out of his grace.

---

[1] Lit. *ashamed*, but there is probably an error in the text.

[2] It is probable that the Armenian translator has confused and perhaps amplified the passage. The printed Vulgate has 'the angel of the Lord,' but a 12th century Codex of Paris, written by a certain Nerses, has 'the Spirit of the Lord.'

p. 171 (c. ix. 8) (Ephr.). For that reason he then raised him up into the third heaven in an inscrutable way and taught him ἀπόῤῥητα in supernatural wise...but instantly Saul rose afresh from the ground and [with open eyes, saw no one...by his hand they took him and brought him to Damascus] whither he set out to go so proudly...

p. 172 (c. ix 10) (Ephr.). The Lord was revealed in a vision by night to Ananias, that without fear he might come and baptise the persecutor. It (?) again was revealed to Saul, that without hesitation he might awake in presence of his physician.

p. 184 (ix. 27) (Ephr.). But as he was persecuted by the Jews who were there, and as he was not trusted by the disciples who were there, for they did not, he says, believe that he was a disciple; then Barnabas presented him to all his companions who were in Jerusalem, took him by the hand and led him to the Apostles.

p. 195 (c. x. 11, 12) as in the Armenian Vulgate.

p. 201 (c. x. 34 from εἶπεν to 35) as in Armenian Vulgate, then the comment " that also among the heathen who to us seemed despicable, if there be found one who worships him truly, he is acceptable before him."

p. 205 (c. x.) (Ephr.). While then Peter having come in, recounted the preaching of our Lord, whence and where he began and where he finished by the Cross, and about his resurrection and about the 40 days that he remained and afterwards ascended, and that all the prophets witness to him, and that every one is forgiven who believes and is baptised in his name; so on the spot the Holy Spirit came by means of tongues and settled on all the hearers of the word, and they began to speak with tongues, as the course of the history shews.

p. 230 (c. xii. 19) (Ephr.). [But Herod, when he sought him and found him not, having asked the guards ordered them to be slain.]

p. 256 (c. xiv. 20) as in the Arm. Vulgate. Then the comment "when the day declined and it became dark, the disciples brought him into the city[1].

---

[1] Cf. Fleury "*cum recessisset* populus vespere," and the Sahidic version.

p. 257 (c. xiv. 23) as in Arm. Vulgate, and the following comment:

Mark the power of the Gospel. For in those very cities whence they drove them out along with their gospelling which they preached, lo! they made elders and deacons fearlessly.

p. 262 (c. xv. 6) and since there was a great dispute between the synagogue and the heathen[1] and with the Apostles and their friends, the Apostles came and gathered together and the priests along with the multitude to see what issue would come forth about this subject (λόγον). [And after much discussion Peter stood up and said to them]: for Paul stood forward in Jerusalem before Simeon and his companions against the law, as also he spoke in Antioch before them against the keeping of the law. But this Simeon, who was silent in Antioch, when Paul came forward and spoke against the law in Jerusalem, there dwelt in him the Holy Spirit[2], and he began to speak against the upholders of the law thus :...

p. 277 (c. xv. 29 ?). For as you shall keep faithfully all this without circumcision and observation of the law, ye shall receive the Holy Spirit to speak all tongues[3]; even as your companions received, the party of Cornelius, who were chosen before you.

p. 289 (c. xvi. 9). So then that they may hasten to come to Macedonia, where things were ready for them, there appeared to Paul as it were[4] a man of Macedonia, for he came and prayed and besought him to come and help in Macedonia (after which c. xvi. 10—12 as in Arm. Vulg. except Philippopolis for Philippi[5]).

p. 294 (c. xvi. 19). And instead of the price of healing which

---

[1] It looks as if this were meant for 'the synagogue of the Gentiles,' in which case we have a suggestion of the double deputation from Antioch to Jerusalem which appears in Codex Bezae.

[2] We have here something like the text of Codex Bezae

ἀνέcΤΗϹΕΝ ΕΝ π͞ΝΙ Πέτρος.

[3] Does this imply the equivalent of φερόμενοι ἐν τῷ ἁγίῳ πνεύματι in the text?

[4] The ὡσεὶ of Codex Bezae.

[5] So some MSS. of the Arm. Vulg.

the masters of the girl owed to Paul, they stirred up the city against him and accused him of the laws of the Jews which he did not preach to them.

p. 296 (c. xvi. 22, 23) (Chrys. Ephr.). From καὶ οἱ στρατηγοί to τηρεῖν αὐτούς acc. to Arm. Vulg. (but add αὐτούς after ῥαβδίζειν). Then the commentary thus: The heads of the city in rending their garments wished to quiet the tumult of the crowd. They tried to prevent it. Because they saw the crowd set on in fury they wished to quiet their rage by the scourging. And to please the will of the crowd which was collected they pinioned the party of Paul and had them cast into the prison, and gave order to keep them carefully, wishing later on to hear about their cause.

p. 299 (c. xvi. 27) (Ephr.). Then there was a shock in the city and the doors of the prison were opened, and the bonds of the prisoners fell off them. But that there might be no sorrow to the gaoler who was about to believe, none of them fled. For because of this the gaoler deserved the baptism of the font along with his household as he says [then c. xvi. 27—31 as in Arm. Vulg.]...

Then follow vv. 31—35 acc. to Arm. Vulg. On v. 35 the comm. is as follows:

Perhaps the heads of the army knew all the great wonders[1] which had occurred, and so they did not venture of themselves to release them, but sent to the gaoler to dismiss them as it were by stealth.

p. 301 (Ephr.). The Astaritai (= στρατηγοί) were afraid and full of fear, they the mighty of the city, of the earthquake; and knew truly that this earthquake happened[2] on account of them, but they did not undertake to avow it (? = ὁμολογεῖν ἐν αὐτῷ). They sent secretly to bring them out.

Then vv. 35—37 acc. to Arm. Vulgate.

p. 302 (c. xvi. 39) (Ephr.). So then that this favour might

---

[1] It seems to be Chrysostom (ed. Savile iv. 811), but cf. Cod. D,

ΚΑΙ ΑΝΑΜΝΗСΘΕΝΤΕС
ΤΟΝ СΕΙСΜΟΝ ΤΟΝ ΓΕΓΟΝΟΤΑ ΕΦΟΒΗΘΗСΑΝ.

[2] τὸν σεισμὸν τὸν γεγονότα (D).

be unto them, they came[1] and besought of them, (saying), We knew not that ye were just[2]: even as the earthquake indeed presaged about you. So then we ask of you this favour, depart from this city, lest the same men gather together after the earthquake against you, (the same) who before the earthquake were gathered together[3].

p. 310 (c. xvii. 14) (Ephr.). So he came as far as the sea shore, receding[4]. But the Holy Spirit prevented him from preaching, lest they should slay him[5]. [And those who conducted Paul, led him as far as Athens, and having received] from Paul[6] [a command to Silas and Timothy that they should at once come to him] in Athens. [And they went] to him when they received the command[7].

[1] Cod. D.

ΠΑΡΑΓΕΝΟΜΕΝΟΙ.

[2] Cod. D.

ΗΓΝΟΗϹΑΜΕΝ ΤΑ ΚΑΘ ΥΜΑϹ
ΟΤΙ ΕϹΤΑΙ ΑΝΔΡΕϹ ΔΙΚΑΙΟΙ.

[3] Cod. D.

ΠΑΡΕΚΑΛΕϹΑΝ ΑΥΤΟΥϹ ΛΕΓΟΝΤΕϹ
ΕΚ ΤΗϹ ΠΟΛΕΩϹ ΤΑΥΤΗϹ ΕΞΕΛΘΑΤΕ
ΜΗΠΟΤΕ ΠΑΛΙΝ ϹΥΝϹΤΡΑΦѠϹΙΝ ΗΜΕΙΝ
ΕΠΙΚΡΑΖΟΝΤΕϹ ΚΑΘ ΥΜѠΝ.

[4] Cod. D.

ΑΠΕΛΘΕΙΝ ΕΠΙ ΤΗΝ ΘΑΛΑϹϹΑΝ
abire ad mare uersus.

[5] Cod. D.

ΠΑΡΗΛΘΕΝ ΔΕ ΤΗΝ ΘΕϹϹΑΛΙΑΝ
ΕΚѠΛΥΘΗ ΓΑΡ ΕΙϹ ΑΥΤΟΥϹ
ΚΗΡΥΞΑΙ ΤΟΝ ΛΟΓΟΝ.

[6] Cod. D.

ΛΑΒΟΝΤΕϹ ΔΕ ΕΝΤΟΛΗΝ ΠΑΡΑ ΠΑΥΛΟΥ.

[7] The words 'and they went to him' are due to the arrangement of the text in the Bezan Greek, which runs

ΠΡΟϹ ΤΟΝ ϹΕΙΛΑΝ ΚΑΙ ΤΙΜΟΘΕΟΝ
ΟΠѠϹ ΕΝ ΤΑΧΕΙ ΕΛΘѠϹΙΝ
ΠΡΟϹ ΑΥΤΟΝ ΕΞΗΕϹΑΝ
=ad eum proficiscebantur.

The last line has been detached from the previous ones by the reader or translator, and made into a separate sentence. If this is the correct explanation (and it is almost certain in view of the absence of the verb ἐξῃεσαν in the rendering of the previous sentence), then we have again an instance of the early currency of the Bezan line-division.

p. 329 (c. xviii. 17) (Ephr.).   "The believing Greeks beat
Sosthenes the head of the Synagogue"...and that the governor
when he saw it might not require vengeance of the in-
dignity offered to him, i.e. to Sosthenes, he became as though
he saw not, that their blows might be redoubled yet more[1].

p. 331 (c. xviii. 19, 20) (Ephr.).   So Paul came and arrived
at Ephesus and with him Aquila's party and he spoke there in
the Synagogue.   And they asked him to remain with them;
but he did not choose to stay longer with them; because
whither he was concerned (to go) thither he had to go.   However he did not simply leave them, but with a promise again
that they should expect his coming by the will of God.   This
he says, that they may pray God for his coming, that He may
will it.

p. 334 (c. xix. 1) (Ephr.).   Paul wished of his own will to go
to Jerusalem; but the Spirit sent him back to Asia[2], as he
relates; [it came to pass], he says [while Apollo was in Corinth,
Paul went round the upper regions and came down to Ephesus
and found certain of the disciples and said to them: If ye
received the Holy Spirit in believing.   But they say, But not
even if the Holy Spirit is have we heard etc.] as far as v. 7,
inclusive acc. to Arm. Vulg., only reading κ. Ιησου Χριστου v. 5.

p. 340 (c. xix. 15) (Ephr.).   You, he says, mutilated and
broken-backed by the devils, who are you who bid the devils
depart?   And the devil straitened (= συνέστελλε) them right
and left and drove them forth from the house.

p. 352 (c. xix. 38, 39) (Ephr.).   This Demetrius[3], vile and

---

[1] This involves the reading of D *tunc gallio fingebat eum non uidere.* Cf. the
Fleury text: *et gallio simulabat se non uidere.*

[2] Cod. D.

ΘΕΛΟΝΤΟC ΔΕ ΤΟΥ ΠΑΥΛΟΥ
ΚΑΤΑ ΤΗΝ ΙΔΙΑΝ ΒΟΥΛΗΝ
ΠΟΡΕΥΕCΘΑΙ ΕΙC ΙΕΡΟCΟΛΥΜΑ
ΕΙΠΕΝ ΑΥΤΩ ΤΟ Π͞Ν͞Α ΥΠΟCΤΡΕΦΕΙΝ ΕΙC ΤΗΝ ΑCΙΑΝ.

[3] Cod. D.

ΕΙ ΜΕΝ ΟΥΝ ΔΗΜΗΤΡΙΟC ΟΥΤΟC
ΟΙ ΚΑΙ CΥΝ ΑΥΤΩ ΤΕΧΝΕΙΤΕ.

shameless, he says, and the children (παῖδες) of his craft, if they have any suit with one another[1], let them stand forward and make it clear to the hegemon. And [if there be] any other[2] [enquiry, let] it be [pronounced on in the lawful assembly].

p. 354 (c. xx. 3) (Ephr.). According to the Armenian Vulgate, and then as follows: For that the Jews plotted against him, he wished to go into Syria, but the Spirit turned him back into Macedonia[3].

p. 356 (c. xx. 7) (Ephr.). For as Paul was speaking from dawn until midnight, the youth fell asleep and fell from three stories, because he was sitting there; and gave up the ghost. But Paul went down, fell on him and restored him to life, as he relates. After which vv. 8—11 inclusive according to the Armenian Vulgate.

p. 363 (c. xx. 24) (Ephr.). When he began to tell truly what he was to undergo in Jerusalem from priests and scribes, but he for the sake of the saints who were in Jerusalem was going to comfort them; and again, that he taught, if ill-treatment does not appal him, then without scruple or fear, without shrinking, he was hastening forward to meet difficulties. Nevertheless he adds this saying: non aestimata mihi anima mea pretiosior quam labores Evangelii vitae et quam ministerium Evangelii verbi quod a domino nostro recepi, id est, testimonium dabo Judaeis et Graecis[4].

p. 410 (c. xxiv.) (Ephr.). When the Rhetor spoke about the peace of their people, and about the disturbance which in all places Paul excited against them, then an order came to Paul to make a defence of himself. (Then c. xxiv. 10 as far as ἐπι-

---

[1] Cod. D.

    εχογcιν προc αγτογc τινα λογον.

[2] Cod. D.

    ει Δε περι ετερων επιzητειτε.

[3] Cf. D.

    και γενηθειc αγτω επιβογλнc γπο των ιογΔαιων
    нθελнcεν αναχθнναι ειc cγριαν
    ειπεν Δε το π̄ν̄ᾱ αγτω γποcτρεφειν
    Δια τнc ΜακεΔονιαc.

[4] Observe the agreement in the concluding words with Cod. Bezae:

    Διαμαρτγραcθαι ιογΔαιοιc και ελλнcιν

στάμενος acc. to Arm. Vulg.) Therefore Paul was no stranger or new comer, if he had known the judge for many years.

p. 410 (c. xxiv. 11) (Ephr.). But he stood forward and said : They have accounted me a raving maniac and a disturber of the synagogue. Be cognisant, O hegemon, that in this city I am but a few days and not any considerable number. And in the temple, as I was worshipping, they came and found me, I will not say a crowd mustered apart ; I was teaching. So then if in their synagogue outside the city or here in the city they could not catch me and find me teaching a crowd mustered together, how where all these events were not found, do they come and accuse me as an impostor[1] ?

p. 411 (c. xxiv. 14) (Ephr.). However though I were even a Christian, as they say, yet I also worship the God of our fathers, the family of Abraham who without the law worshipped God. So that I believe in the law and in the prophets, whatsoever is written.

p. 439 (c. xxvii. 23) (Ephr.). Paul told them about the angel who appeared to him and said to him : Before the Caesar thou art to stand and your ship is broken, and not one man of the 270 men in it shall be lost.

After which vv. 27—32 acc. to Arm. Vulg.

p. 454 (c. xxviii. 30) (Ephr.). And he was a space of two years in all at his own expense, and received all who came in unto him. So when (ὡς) he discoursed to Jews from dawn till night about Christ from the law and prophets and reiterated about the unfaithful who received not the words of Isaiah; Luke turned and remembered his actions and the labours of his hands, which he gave as hire of his house for one biennium[2]. And that he ceased not to discourse about Christ

---

[1] The Armenian literally.

[2] This apparently inexplicable sentence means, I suspect, that there was a gloss in the text concerning the cloak and books, which Paul left in Troas (2 Tim. iv. 13), and used them to pay for the rent of the Roman lodging. The word 'actions' stands for the Syriac ܪܠܝܢܐܩ, and this is a misreading of the transliterated Greek φελόνη. (The Peshito, however, makes it a book-case ܪܟܬܐ ܒܝܬ ; as of course, it might be ; cf. Birt, *Das antike Buchwesen*, p. 65) The Philoxenian transliterate ܦܝܠܘܢܐ.

to Jews and heathen, who went out and came in to him. And he was saying that Jesus Christ is the son of God[1]. For for his sake we labour and attain to crowns by means of Christ.

That Ephrem really imagined the house was to be paid for by the proceeds of the cloak and books, may be seen from the following extract from the prologue to 2 Tim. in Ephrem's Comm. on the Pauline Epp.

"Penulam (*phighon*, evidently from a Syriac transliteration) autem et libros iussit afferre, aut ut venditis illis, *perderet pro domo conducta* · aut ut haereditare faceret, cui iustum esset."

This reference in Ephrem on the Pauline epistles renders almost certain our explanation of the obscure passage in Ephrem on the Acts.

[1] Cf. the Philoxenian text, and the Latin codd. *tol.* and *dem· dov.*

CORSSEN AND BLASS ON THE WESTERN TEXT
OF THE ACTS.

Let us now try, before proceeding to examine Mr Chase's theory of the Syriac influence on the Western text, to get some idea of the results which have been arrived at, and the prospects of further conclusions which are being held out to us, by two distinguished German scholars, one of whom approaches the subject from the side of the Latin versions, and the other from that of the recensions of the Greek. We will begin with Corssen's Programm, entitled 'The Cyprianic text of the Acts of the Apostles'[1]. As there is probably no living scholar who is more familiar with the Old Latin texts of the Bible, nor one who knows better how to present his reasonings and results, we shall be sure to get some daylight on the Western question from this tract, although it is only a preliminary notice of further enquiries and is contained in less than 30 pages. Corssen begins by drawing attention to the importance of the Fleury palimpsest from which Sabatier published in 1743 a couple of fragments of the Acts[2] and which has, after various attempts by other transcribers, been lately published in what is probably a final textual form by Samuel Berger[3]. The value of this version (of which one can only deplore that more leaves have not been preserved) lies in the fact of its being an Old Latin rendering, presumably of a Greek text which must have been in singular agreement with the text of Codex Bezae. It

---

[1] Peter Corssen: *Der Cyprianische Text der Acta Apostolorum*. Berlin, Weidmannsche Buchhandlung, 1892.

[2] Quoted as *reg* in Tischendorf's Apparatus.

[3] Berger. *Le Palimpseste de Fleury*. Paris, 1889.

becomes, therefore, a textual authority of the highest importance, not only on account of the support which it gives to the Bezan text, and the help which it occasionally furnishes where that text is *in lacuna*, but also because it is suspected of being often more archaic than Codex Bezae itself.

Further, as Corssen points out, the Fleury Latin is in the Acts of the Apostles in close agreement with the quotations of Cyprian, and other Latin fathers whose text is related to that of Cyprian, so that it becomes possible to restore by skilful editing a large part of what Corssen calls the Cyprianic text of the Acts.   We thus obtain a Latin text of the Acts, not merely of the sixth century, to which period the Fleury MS. may be referred, but at least, according to Corssen, of the middle of the third.   The importance of this is obvious, and we shall probably be able to shew that Corssen's estimate of the age of the restored text is too modest.   It must go back farther than Cyprian.

The argument by which the antiquity of the text is demonstrated depends upon a comparison of the readings of the Fleury text with (i) the quotations of Cyprian, (ii) with similar quotations in two works of Augustine entitled *De Actis cum Felice Manichaeo* and *Contra epistulam Manichaei*, (iii) with the quotations made in a work of the fifth century, wrongly attributed to Prosper, and entitled *De promissionibus et praedicationibus Dei*.   From a comparison of these various texts, Corssen shews their derivation from a common Latin primitive, which he calls the Cyprianic text.   And this common primitive was a text which had an internal unity and sequence which we look for in vain in the text of Codex Bezae, however much we may be persuaded that the Cyprianic text agreed in the main with the peculiarities of the Bezan Greek.   That is to say, the restored Cyprianic text is a Western witness of greater worth than even the Greek of Codex Bezae.

Corssen then proceeds to suggest that the text of Codex Bezae is composite, and can be resolved into an original Western text *plus* certain contaminations and insertions which are due to the influence of the Common Greek text.   In order to make this clearer we will reproduce Corssen's first and leading illustration. The opening verses of the Acts in the two tracts of Augustine against the Manichees agree in the rendering

> in die quo apostolos elegit per spiritum
> sanctum et praecepit praedicare evangelium.

This, according to Corssen, was the primitive rendering; its influence may be seen in an extract from Vigilius *Contra Varimadum*

> in die qua apostolos elegit per spiritum
> sanctum praedicare evangelium,

and, with some re-action from the common text in Augustine's *De Unitate ecclesiae,*

> usque in diem, quo apostolos elegit per spiritum
> sanctum mandans eis praedicare evangelium.

But if this be the primitive form, we arrive at the important conclusion that it cannot have been made from the text of D as it now stands, for while the restored Cyprianic text is the equivalent of a Greek text

> ἄχρι ἧς ἡμέρας
> ἐξελέξατο τοὺς ἀποστόλους
> διὰ πνεύματος ἁγίου
> καὶ ἐκέλευσε
> κηρύσσειν τὸ εὐαγγέλιον

the text of D is

> ἄχρι ἧς ἡμέρας
> ἀνελήμφθη ἐντειλάμενος τοῖς ἀποστόλοις
> διὰ πνεύματος ἁγίου οὓς ἐξελέξατο καὶ ἐκέλευσε
> κηρύσσειν τὸ εὐαγγέλιον.

This latter text is, according to Corssen, due to the influence upon the equivalent of the Cyprianic text of the common Greek text

> ἄχρι ἧς ἡμέρας
> ἐντειλάμενος τοῖς ἀποστόλοις
> διὰ πνεύματος ἁγίου
> οὓς ἐξελέξατο
> ἀνελήμφθη.

We are therefore to regard the text of Codex Bezae as made up out of (i) a primitive Western text (call it the β-text) corrupted by mixture with the common text (which we will call the a-text). According to this theory the words καὶ ἐκέλευσε κηρύσσειν τὸ εὐαγγέλιον are not a mere gloss on the common text from some outside source, as they certainly seem to be at the first examination, but a part of an early redaction of the text of the Acts which does not agree with the common text[1].

The first thing that we have to reflect upon is the way in which Corssen restores the Cyprianic text in this passage. We will add something to the demonstration of the antiquity of the words which have been apparently appended to the primitive text by Codex Bezae, and we will do something to justify the apparent absurdity of the text restored by Corssen, which makes the choice of the Apostles take place on Ascension day. In the first place, there is evidence earlier than Cyprian of the currency of the words

καὶ ἐκέλευσε κηρύσσειν τὸ εὐαγγέλιον.

In the 21st chapter of his Apology, Tertullian speaks of the Ascension as follows:

ad quadraginta dies egit docens eos quae docerent. Dehinc ordinatis eis ad officium praedicandi per orbem, circumfusa nube in caelum est receptus.

We have here the trace of the commission *to preach* in an account of the Ascension and notice that it is like the added words in Codex Bezae, in that, although the account is in the main that of the Acts, it is connected with the terms of Mark xvi. 15; and there can be little doubt that Tertullian in his text of the Ascension had at least the equivalent of the word κηρύσσειν. But in the second place, the peculiar language

ordinatis eis ad officium praedicandi

---

[1] Corssen points out in a foot-note that I have, in my Study of Codex Bezae, missed the explanation of the genesis of the variants, through a failure to detect the reconstruction which D exhibits of an archaic text under the influence of the received text. Possibly this may be so, but we are not yet quite convinced on this point.

seems to imply something more than the equivalent of ἐν-
τειλάμενος or ἐκέλευσεν; it is almost as strong as *elegit ad
praedicandum;* but, if this be the case, Tertullian's text would
be uncommonly like that which we have found restored by
Corssen, for it involves the election of the Apostles on the
day of the Ascension. We may say, then, that there is a very
high probability that Tertullian had in his text of the Acts
the injunction *to preach;* and a lesser probability that he had
words which implied the Apostolic election as occurring on the
day of the Ascension. So that something can be said in favour
of the antiquity of Corssen's restoration ; and I, for my part,
am quite satisfied that the supposed gloss in the Western text
is earlier than the time of Tertullian. We will give another
little illustration of the way in which the Fleury text and its
companions can be put in evidence for the existence of a
Latin translation of the story of the Ascension earlier than
Tertullian.

The manner in which Tertullian quotes the verses Acts i.
10, 11 implies, at all events in certain touches, something more
than his own habitually free renderings of the text : we have
as follows :

De Resurr. c. 22. Quis caelo descendentem *talem* conspexit,
qualem ascendentem apostoli viderant secundum angelorum
constitutum ?

Ibid. c. 51. Idem tamen et substantia et forma qua
ascendit, *talis* etiam descensurus, ut angeli adfirmant.

Adversus Praxeam c. 30. Hic et venturus est rursus super
nubes caeli, *talis qualis* et ascendit.

It will be noticed that in these three passages Tertullian
harps upon the words *talis* and *qualis.* I infer that they were
known to him in a Latin translation of the Acts : (the Vulgate
and most other fathers have *sic veniet quemadmodum,* which is
a more literal rendering). If we now turn to the Fleury
palimpsest, and examine its reading of Apoc. i. 7, we have

et uidebunt eum omnes tribus terrae *talem.*

The added word *talem* is not a mere blunder of the Fleury
text : the Fleury text is in the Apocalypse the same as that of

Primasius and Cyprian, and is used by Haussleiter to restore the so-called Cyprianic Apocalypse, just as Corssen wishes to use it for the editing of the Cyprianic Acts.   When we turn to the text of the Acts used by Primasius, as edited by Haussleiter, we find

<blockquote>et uidebit eum omnis terra talem.</blockquote>

It is impossible to resist the conclusion that the primitive Latin Apocalypse in very early days had talem in its text, perhaps as the remains of a primitive gloss, something like Tertullian's talem qualem ascendentem apostoli viderant or talem qualis ascendit.   But such a text must be held to be assimilated to that of a passage in the Latin Acts.   The commentary of Primasius does not help us to restore the missing clause; it has talem hidden away amongst the explanation of the author, but it does not seem as if more than this were in Primasius' text, for he has made an expansion of his own, cum talem viderint qualem non credebant[1].

But even if it should be maintained that talem is a corruption of amen, which occurs a little later in the text, the error is still due to the influence of the passage in the Acts, and implies the word talem in Acts i. 11.   If this reasoning be of any force, we must again say that the restored Cyprianic text is earlier than Cyprian.   It might just as well be called Tertullianic.

Even where we cannot carry a gloss back with certainty into the Latin of Tertullian, we can shew sometimes that the gloss itself was known to him, without determining the form in which he read it.   For example in Apology c. 39 we have

<blockquote>itaque qui animo animaque miscemur, nihil de rei communicatione dubitamus; omnia indiscreta apud nos praeter uxores.</blockquote>

The first sentence is an obvious paraphrase of καρδία καὶ ψυχὴ μία in Acts iv. 32 and the last is the equivalent of ἀλλ'

---

[1] The whole passage is "Et uidebit illum omnis terra.   Omnes etiam terreni uel omnes generaliter mali, maxime Judaei, qui eum ut minimum putavere necandum, cum talem uiderint qualem non credebant, sera semetipsos poenitentia lamentabuntur, et plangent se adveniente eo.   Ita amen."

ἦν αὐτοῖς πάντα κοινά in the same verse. The intermediate sentence is, therefore, a reproduction of the Bezan gloss

$$καὶ οὐκ ἦν διάκρισις ἐν αὐτοῖς οὐδεμία,$$

but whether it comes from the Greek, or from a Latin rendering

et non erat dubitatio in eis ulla

we cannot tell.

But the gloss must have been known to Tertullian, and have stood in the same place which it occupies in the Bezan text.

Other instances of the same kind may readily be brought forward; for example in *De Pudicitia*, c. 21

In illa disceptatione custodiendae necne legis primus omnium Petrus spiritu instinctus et de nationum vocatione praefatus: Et nunc, inquit, cur tentastis etc.

Here *spiritu instinctus* is due to the gloss in the Bezan text of Acts xv. 7

$$ἀνέστησεν ἐν \overline{πνι} πέτρος$$

primus omnium may be due to a similar gloss in Acts ii. 14 where the situation is similar, ἐπῆρεν πρῶτος τὴν φωνὴν αὐτοῦ. Even where the text of Tertullian is not under the influence of Bezan glosses, it sometimes gives us the key to the genesis of the glosses.

For example, in *De Baptismate* c. 10

quoniam qui Joannis baptismum habebant non accepissent spiritum sanctum, quem nc auditu quidem noverant,

the language of Tertullian suggests to us the following primitive and idiomatic rendering of Acts xix. 2

sed ne auditu quidem spiritum sanctum accepimus.

Now compare with this the Bezan confusion,

ΑΛΛ ΟΥΔΕ $\overline{ΠΝΑ}$ ΑΓΙΟΝ [ΛΑΜΒΑΝΟΥCΙ
ΤΙΝΕC] ΗΚΟΥCΑΜΕΝ

= sed neque $\overline{spm}$ sanctum [accipiunt quidam] audivimus.

And it is not unreasonable to suppose that the *accipiunt quidam* of the Bezan text goes back into *quidem accepimus*, and that the attempt to bring the translation and text into closer harmony with one another has led to the Bezan conflation and confusion.

Returning now to Corssen, and his theory that the original form of the Western text has been mixed with the common text, we remark that the theory is an attractive one in so far as it furnishes an explanation of the structure of a number of passages that appear double in D, but it is encumbered by the difficulty that it does not furnish a single explanation of any residual Western variations. The text is thus, from Corssen's view, a double redaction, the reason for whose variation must be sought in the sources.

The following specimens are given by Corssen to illustrate the double redaction:

Acts iii. 7, 8.

Text. rec.

καὶ πιάσας αὐτὸν τῆς δεξιᾶς χειρὸς ἤγειρεν αὐτὸν
παραχρῆμα δὲ ἐστερεώθησαν
αἱ βάσεις αὐτοῦ καὶ τὰ σφυδρὰ
καὶ ἐξαλλόμενος ἔστη
καὶ περιεπάτει

with which cf. D

καὶ πιάσας αὐτὸν τῆς δεξιᾶς χειρὸς ἤγειρεν
καὶ παραχρῆμα ἐστάθη
καὶ ἐστερεώθησαν αὐτοῦ
αἱ βάσεις καὶ τὰ σφυρὰ [καὶ ἐξαλλόμενος ἔστη]
καὶ περιεπάτει χαιρόμενος

the bracketed words being assumed to be borrowed from the common text.

The Fleury text agrees closely with D, as follows: (italics where the text is illegible or doubtful)

Et adpraehensa manu *eius dextera*
excitauit eum
et continuo stetit

> confirm*atique* sunt
> gressus eius et laccania
> et ambulabat *gaudens* et exultans

where observe that the Fleury text has no trace of the words which Corssen considers an interpolation from the common text.

Or we may take Acts xviii. 8, where Text. rec. has

> καὶ πολλοὶ τῶν Κορινθίων
> ἀκούοντες ἐπίστευον
> καὶ ἐβαπτίζοντο

and D

> καὶ πολλοὶ τῶν Κορινθίων
> ἀκούοντες [ἐπίστευον
> καὶ] ἐβαπτίζοντο πιστεύοντες τῷ θεῷ
> διὰ τοῦ ὀνόματος τοῦ $\overline{κυ}$ ἡμῶν $\overline{ιην}$ $\overline{χρυ}$

and the Fleury text

> et *quomodo multa* plebs corinthiorum
> audierant uerbum $\overline{dni}$
> *unti sunt* credentes
> in nomine $\overline{ihu}$ $\overline{χρι}$

where again the text of the palimpsest has not the repetition which characterises D, and may perhaps be regarded as an earlier form of the Western text.

There can be no doubt that the Bezan text is marked by such doublets as Corssen points out, whatever may be their origin, and that whether they consist of whole sentences or occasional words, one of the first things necessary for the clearing of the Bezan text is the separation of the doublets.

For example Acts xix. 8 (D)

> εἰσελθὼν δὲ ὁ Παῦλος εἰς τὴν συναγωγὴν
> ἐν δυνάμει μεγάλῃ ἐπαρρησιάζετο

is probably the resultant of two texts; the (*a*) text

> εἰσελθὼν δὲ εἰς τὴν συναγωγὴν
> ἐπαρρησιάζετο

and the (β) text

> εἰσελθὼν δὲ ὁ Παῦλος εἰς τὴν συναγωγὴν
> ἐν δυνάμει μεγάλῃ ἐλάλει (?)

So in Acts iii. 13 the text of D

> κατὰ πρόσωπον Πειλάτου
> τοῦ κρείναντος ἐκείνου
> ἀπολύειν αὐτὸν θέλοντος

should be resolved into the α-text,

> κατὰ πρόσωπον Πειλάτου
> κρίναντος ἐκείνου ἀπολύειν

and the β-text

> κατὰ πρόσωπον Πειλάτου
> θέλοντος ἐκείνου
> ἀπολύειν αὐτόν

The difficulty here would be that the Fleury text has 'cum ille iudicaret eum dimittere'; the text avoids the doublet, but sides with the α-text, instead of presenting the desiderated β-text.

In the same way Acts xx. 18 (D)

> ὡς δὲ παρεγένοντο πρὸς αὐτὸν
> ὅμως ἐόντων αὐτῶν εἶπεν πρὸς αὐτοὺς

should be resolved into the α-text

> ὡς δὲ παρεγένοντο πρὸς αὐτὸν
> εἶπεν αὐτοῖς

and the β-text

> καὶ ὅμως ἐόντων αὐτῶν
> εἶπεν πρὸς αὐτούς.

(Here again the Fleury text is absent; it is significant that the Gigas MS., which represents the text of Lucifer, is double and reads " cum convenissent ad eum simulque essent.")

It is not surprising that after suggesting this means of purifying the text of D, of whose base he has justified the antiquity, Corssen should say some significant things about the

modern edited texts of the Acts, which he declares to be the
reflected images of a fourth-century recension, which itself is
arbitrary in character. We build, says he, on the great uncials,
as if they were rocks! Such language as this would, in England,
be credited to a disciple of Burgon, and set aside as mere
fanaticism. But it would hardly be wise to treat Corssen with
that kind of contempt.

Upon the whole we should say that the value of Corssen's
Programm consists chiefly in the demonstration it furnishes
of the antiquity of the Western Latin, but that further investigation is necessary before we could say decidedly that the
β-text had existed in Greek, unmixed with the a-text. It
needs to be shewn that the β-text is something more than the
possible contamination of a text by a version[1].

Precisely at this point of difficulty, Blass comes forward
with a learned and acute investigation of the essential double-
ness of the early text of the Acts in which he tries to detach
the Bezan base from the received text with which it has been
encumbered, and to justify the text so detached as in linguistic
harmony with the language of the New Testament in general
and of S. Luke in particular.

Blass's theory is that it is significant that the Western
variations are most intense in the writings of S. Luke, and that
it is a natural assumption to make that two copies of the
author's works got into circulation, the rougher and earlier
of which (the β-text) is represented to us approximately in the
Codex Bezae, the Fleury-text, and the marginal annotations of
the Heraclean Syriac (which are translated from a Greek MS.)
together with sundry survivals in other texts and versions.

The supposition that the Western text makes no material
addition to our knowledge is held by Blass to be a mistake;
we cannot explain all the Western expansions of the Acts by
carelessness and harmonistic corruption; but if this be so, the
Western tradition acquires at once a certain independence.

---

[1] Corssen's attempt to restore the text of the vision of Ananias in c. ix.
10—12, and to reduce it to a mere subjective impression of S. Paul's own
inner experience, does not need any serious treatment; for, as Blass says,
'Who performed the baptism?'

The scribe and translator give place to the author. Accordingly Blass proceeds to analyse and justify the Western peculiarities, beginning with the tenth chapter of the Acts and working forward through the tract where the glosses are most significant, and then returning to read the first nine chapters in the light obtained from the study of the rest of the book, the linguistic analysis of which is often extremely suggestive.

The originality of some of the Western expansions of the text ought, I think, to be at least provisionally conceded; it is difficult to believe that a mere transcriber invented the 'seven steps' of the prison at Jerusalem which S. Peter and the angel descend together; the detail which is given in the visit of Peter to Cornelius that when they came near to Cesarea, one of the slaves ran forward to announce Peter's approach, and that Cornelius sprang forward to greet him, is as life-like as anything we could wish, and agrees with the statement that Cornelius had sent *two* slaves along with a devout soldier.

The story of the sons of Sceva the priest is free, in the Bezan form, from the contradiction which is involved in speaking of seven sons in the beginning of the story and calling them ἀμφότεροι in the conclusion of it; yet it does not seem as if the Bezan text were a corrupt and late reconstruction reducible on examination to the form of the received text.

The visit of S. Paul to Jerusalem in company with Mnason is obscure enough in the received text, which makes it one day's journey, and yet implies that S. Paul carried his host with him into a city where he had many friends. The Bezan text knows that it is two days' journey (68 miles, as Blass points out), and makes it intelligible why Paul's entertainer on the road should travel with him[1].

The statement that S. Paul lectured every day in Ephesus from 11 a.m. to 4 p.m. (the hours when Tyrannus' school was

---

[1] Many of these Bezan singularities are discussed by Prof. Ramsay in his *Church in the Roman Empire*, and some of them are approved by him as bearing the stamp of originality.

disengaged ?) has every appearance of being a statement based upon direct knowledge[1].

More remarkable still is the fact which Blass points out that the Western glosses occasionally add to what are called the *We-sections* of the Acts.

In Acts xi. 27 the current text tells us that ἐν ταύταις δὲ ταῖς ἡμέραις κατῆλθον ἀπὸ Ἱεροσολύμων προφῆται εἰς Ἀντιόχειαν· ἀναστὰς δὲ εἶς ἐξ αὐτῶν ὀνόματι Ἄγαβος κτέ., to which Codex Bezae adds as follows after Ἀντιόχειαν,

> ἦν δὲ πολλὴ ἀγαλλίασις
> συνεστραμμένων δὲ ἡμῶν
> ἔφη εἶς ἐξ αὐτῶν ὀνόματι Ἄγαβος

where the peculiar form of the second line will be noticed ; whoever the writer is, he has at all events thrown himself pretty vigorously into the situation. Nor is this the only case of the kind, for we find Irenaeus (ed. Mass. 201) quoting amongst the proofs that Luke was the inseparable companion of Paul a passage from the Acts as follows :

" Quoniam autem is Lucas inseparabilis fuit a Paulo et cooperarius eius in Evangelio, ipse facit manifestum, non glorians, sed ab ipsa productus veritate. Separati enim, inquit, a Paulo, et Barnaba et Johanne qui vocabatur Marcus, et cum navigassent Cyprum *nos venimus in Troadem.*" The whole argument of the passage turns on the occurrence of the words *nos venimus* in the text ; and Irenaeus goes on to quote passage after passage from the We-sections in order to shew that Luke was the constant companion of S. Paul, much in the same way as if he were writing an introduction to the Acts for the Cambridge Bible for Schools. I do not see how we can refuse to recognise the existence of the words

> κατηντήσαμεν εἰς Τρῳάδα

in the text of Acts xvi. 7 in Irenaeus. Nor can the reading be very well dissociated from the previous case, since the tendency

---

[1] Mr Chase's theory is that it is an assimilation to the darkness at the Crucifixion, with an hour put on at each end ; I suppose, to make the darkness of S. Paul's teaching more visible ! Are we to take this as a *jeu d'esprit* ?

in both is to intensify the personal element in the narrative. A similar personal touch is preserved in Acts xxvii. 35, where, Cod 137, the obelized Heraclean and the Sahidic add after ἐσθίειν the words ἐπιδιδοὺς καὶ ἡμῖν.

Where shall we find a reviser or glossator earlier than the days of Irenaeus, whose critical faculties were so highly developed as to make all these alterations and expansions in the text, who had travelled so far as to correct and expand the geography at every point, and had studied the history so carefully that he was able to illustrate the text with fresh meanings, and to remove inconsistencies which would hardly have been alluded to in an uncritical age? Can Tatian or the first Syriac translator or reviser be responsible for all this? We admit that if the glossator be a separate person from the author, he must have had the soul of a harmonist, but he must also have been gifted with some of the trained instincts of a modern critic. Such explanations as that of the double persecution at Iconium (Acts xiv.) or the remark that when Paul took up his lodging at the house of Justus, he had left his old friends Aquila and Priscilla (Acts xviii. 7), are of the nature of a modern commentary. Now I am willing to admit that Tatian was something of a commentator, and in my notes on his Diatessaron have shown that this wonderful work may be described from one point of view as the earliest commentary on the New Testament; but the rehandling of the text of the Acts is so much more extensive than the explanatory touches in the Gospels, that one hesitates to say that the Western text is due entirely to Tatian, and to his translation of the New Testament into the Syriac language. It may be so, but the theory of Blass is much easier, which throws back a part at all events of the textual changes upon the author and his sources. And the theory demands the more consideration inasmuch as it is now practically certain that the so-called Cyprianic Latin text cannot be later than the second century, so that any texts or versions which lie behind this must be not very remote from the actual sources.

On every account therefore the Blass-Corssen theory needs to be carefully looked into; even if it be not the true solution

of the textual bifurcation, we must at least allow this much,
that the bifurcation itself is demonstrably so early, that it
would be very unreasonable to suppose that none of the
Western readings were genuine. It may be justified in select
readings even where it cannot be justified as a whole. And
this means that there is nothing against which we need to be so
much on our guard as the seductive supposition that the cause
of certain variants is necessarily the cause of the remainder, or
that we can, because we have explained two or three obscure
changes in the text, use the Newtonian *vera causa* over the
remainder. The Bezan text and all other Western texts will
remain complex until their simplicity has been demonstrated
in a sufficiently broad and comprehensive manner.

The actual test of the correctness of Blass' reconstructions
will be best made by a close study of individual passages ; and,
where it is possible, by setting up the *a*-text and *β*-text side by
side and comparing them with the earliest versions.

For example in Acts xvi. 10 the current text is

> ὡς δὲ τὸ ὅραμα εἶδεν
> εὐθέως ἐζητήσαμεν ἐξελθεῖν εἰς Μακεδονίαν
> συνβιβάζοντες ὅτι προσκέκληται ἡμᾶς ὁ θ̅ς̅
> εὐαγγελίσασθαι αὐτούς.

But Codex Bezae reads

> διεγερθεὶς οὖν διηγήσατο τὸ ὅραμα ἡμῖν
> καὶ ἐνοήσαμεν ὅτι προσκέκληται ἡμᾶς ὁ κ̅ς̅
> εὐαγγελίσασθαι τοὺς ἐν τῇ Μακεδονίᾳ.

Here Blass justifies διεγερθεὶς as a Lucan expression by
Luke viii. 24, and observes that ἐνοήσαμεν, though not Lucan,
is common in the language of the N.T. He points out that the
Sahidic version supports in part the expansion of D, though it
soon falls in line with the received text (*cum autem surrexisset,
narravit nobis visionem ;* statim quaesivimus egredi in Mace-
doniam, ostendentes iis quod Dominus vocaverit nos ad an-
nuntiandum iis evangelium). Further, at the commencement

of the next verse, the β-text gives us a note of time which is wanting in the current text,

$$\tau\hat{\eta} \ \delta\grave{\epsilon} \ \grave{\epsilon}\pi\alpha\acute{\upsilon}\rho\iota\upsilon \ \grave{\alpha}\chi\theta\acute{\epsilon}\upsilon\tau\epsilon\varsigma \ \grave{\alpha}\pi\grave{o} \ \mathrm{T}\rho\omega\acute{\alpha}\delta o\varsigma.$$

The question is, whether all this precision and expansion is due to scribe and commentator. We shall in our next lecture be able to throw a little light upon the subject, though not, perhaps, to come to a complete solution of the questions at issue.

CHARACTER OF THE GLOSSES IN THE WESTERN TEXT OF THE ACTS[1].

We have, in a preceding lecture, completely justified Mr Chase in his hypothesis of an Old Syriac text of the Acts behind the venerable Peshito, and we must now turn for a brief survey of his contention that the hypothesis which we have verified for him is an adequate one to explain the peculiarities of the Western text in general, and of the Bezan Acts in particular.

It will not be possible for us to make a complete examination of a theory which is only partially brought out, and, as we shall show, not very adequately thought out. But we will place ourselves as far as possible in Mr Chase's position, and see whether the glosses look natural and explicable in the light of his hypothesis. When we have done that, we must make a similar attempt to appreciate Dr Blass's view that the Bezan text is a true Lucan text, and the forcible arguments by which he vindicates so many of the expressions in the much abused Codex. Or better, since the investigation is a series of examinations of various passages, we shall try to look at them one by one from every point of view and see whether they suggest Greek, Latin or Syriac individualisms.

Now with regard to the question of Syriasm in the Codex Bezae, I feel sure that no one who had a good knowledge of Semitic languages would read the MS. through without admitting that there were a number of things which were immediately explicable by Syriac influence. Some of these were pointed out in my tract on the Codex Bezae. But at the same time I have no doubt that there would arise a suspicion that other explanations were possible; and further, there would be

---

[1] This lecture was delivered in the Divinity School, Cambridge, January 24, 1894.

a number of textual expansions of which the assumed Semitic scholar would say, "This cannot be credited to any Syriac hand"; and others of which he would say that if they stood for Syriac, it was very bad Syriac.   To take an instance under each head, the first that occur to one's mind, no one would be willing to credit the Syriac language with the addition of the word ἐστιν to the Greek question in Mark v. 9, τί σοι ὄνομά ἐστιν, because a formula of that kind would be in Syriac either

ܡܢ ܫܡܟ or ܐܝܟܢܐ ܫܡܟ

and while we may freely admit that a complete retranslation of the Syriac into Greek or Latin might give the added vocable, the process of glossing an already existing text so as to make up its deficiencies from another text would not give the desired expansion.   Even if we explain it as an assimilation to Luc. viii. 30, the connexion cannot be made through the Syriac. Such a case as this, and numerous parallel cases might be cited for which I refer to my book, must either be a case of primitive variation in the Greek, or it must be a case of Latinisation. Blass would perhaps say the former, though I do not quite know whether he is prepared to extend his theory of a primitive dual text beyond the limits of the Acts and the Gospel of Luke. I should, probably, adhere to my view that it is a case of Latin influence.   But in any case it can hardly be Syriac, unless we assume that a complete new Greek or Latin version was made from the Syriac.

In a similar manner, if we draw attention to the very interesting gloss in Acts xiv. 2,

ο ΔΕ κ̄ϲ̄ ΕΔωΚΕΝ ΤΑχΥ ΕΙΡΗΝΗΝ,

we should hesitate to say 'this is a Syriac gloss,' because the expression in Syriac 'to give peace' means 'to say farewell.' For this reason the translators of the Old Testament have sometimes felt obliged to change the literal rendering of the corresponding Hebrew expression and substitute another word that would be clear of misunderstanding.   For instance, in Numbers xxvi. 6, instead of transferring "the Lord lift up

His face upon thee and give thee peace," the Syriac says
'and make thee peace.' In the same way in 1 Chron. xxii. 9
the words 'and I will give peace and quiet in his days' are
translated 'and peace and tranquillity shall be in his days.'
No doubt these changes in the translation were intended to
remove possible misunderstanding. At first sight then, this
gloss in the Bezan Acts does not look like good Syriac.
Probably Mr Chase would say that the occurrence of the gloss
in the companion document (Codex E) in the form "God made
peace" (ὁ δὲ θς εἰρήνην ἐποίησεν) furnishes the clue to the
underlying Syriac: and of course this may be so; I am only
pointing out that there are a number of things on the face of
the Bezan text which do not look like Syriac at all. Perhaps
that is inevitable in such a complicated enquiry, and where we
know next to nothing of the changes which the documents
have passed through.

But let us assume for a while that Mr Chase's explanation
of the Western variants is the true one, and read the text in
the light of it, and examine carefully some of his illustrations
of the theory. Since all the glosses are in his view Syriac, we
may begin anywhere.

The first thing that we desire to draw attention to is that a
number of the glosses in the Codex Bezae are wrongly inserted,
and the non-appreciation of this palaeographical feature of the
MS. has misled Mr Chase (as well as some other writers) into a
variety of impossible explanations of the meaning and origin of
the glosses. We are to prove first that this displacement of
the glosses is a fact. Let us begin with the interesting gloss at
the close of Acts vi. iu which we are told by the Bezan text

ΚΑΙ ΕΙΔΟΝ ΤΟ ΠΡΟCΩΠΟΝ ΑΥΤΟΥ
ΩCΕΙ ΠΡΟCΩΠΟΝ ΑΓΓΕΛΟΥ
ΕCΤΩΤΟC ΕΝ ΜΕCΩ ΑΥΤΩΝ

where the last line is supposed to be a gloss.

The Latin of the text and gloss is as follows :

et uiderunt faciem eius
quasi faciem angeli
stans in medio eorum.

The gloss appears also in the Fleury palimpsest[1] in the form

> uidebant uultu eius tamquam
> uultum angeli d̄i stantis inter illos

where the variations from the Latin of Codex Bezae must be carefully noted. The Fleury text is generally held to be an independent translation from a Greek text which is in substantial agreement with that of the Codex Bezae; and to furnish evidence that the Bezan Greek is not the solitary phenomenon which it sometimes seems to be. In the present case it follows the Greek of Codex Bezae in translating ἑστῶτος, but it does not render the supposed ἐν μέσῳ αὐτῶν literally, and it adds (if indeed it be an addition) the word *dei* after *angeli*.

Prof. Bernard has recently pointed out that the same gloss on the text is contained in a citation of the passage in an Irish MS., the Leabhar Breac or Speckled Book[2]. He remarks as follows:

'In Acts vi. 15 we have *uidebant...faciem angeli stantis inter illos* which is almost the same as the reading of the Fleury Palimpsest (h) ...*angeli dei stantis inter illos.* The verbal variations here from Codex Bezae (d) = *faciem angeli stans in medio eorum* seem to indicate that this gloss, at all events, originated in the Greek and not in the Latin text.'

We have then two fresh Latin authorities to add to the evidence of Codex Bezae (the only authority for the gloss known to Tischendorf).

Mr Bernard is naturally staggered at the thought that the apparently impossible and ungrammatical reading of the Codex Bezae can be responsible for the grammatical Greek, and for the variant forms of the Latin tradition. We will justify the Bezan Latin presently.

Having now registered the variant forms in which the gloss has come down to us, we ask the question, what possible

---

[1] *reg* of Tischendorf; *h* of Hort.

[2] *Transactions of the Royal Irish Academy.* Vol. xxx. Pt. viii , p. 322.

motive can be assigned to the expansion in question? If we cannot answer the enquiry 'Who made the gloss?' we ought at all events to be able to assign some motive for the conduct of the anonymous scribe and to say why he made it. To this enquiry two answers are made. Prof. Blass counts the passage as one of those in which the primitive dual redaction of the Acts can be recognized; and praises the gloss, which is really a part of St Luke's own text, on account of the vividness which it obviously imparts to the account[1].

The other explanation is that of Mr Chase and is as follows:

"The last line is an interpolation, due to assimilation to xxiv. 21 where the Greek is ἐν αὐτοῖς ἑστώς but the Syriac Vulgate has

ܒܪ ܩܐܡ ܐܝܟ ܒܝܢܬܗܘܢ

The word ܒܝܢܬܗܘܢ is used to translate ἐν μέσῳ αὐτῶν in Matt. xviii. 2, 20, Lc. xxiv. 36. Note the order of the words in the Bezan gloss and in the Syriac of xxiv. 21. The Greek gloss must therefore be the rendering of an old Syriac gloss."

The reader will, of course, turn to Acts xxiv. 21 in order to see whether there is any possible reason for the reference made by Mr Chase's Syriac glossator. He will look for 'the angel' who is glossed and not find him; nor will he be able to make any connexion between the language of St Paul about himself in the xxivth chapter, and the language of St Luke about St Stephen in the vith. In fact, there *is* no connexion between the two passages, and one can only conclude that Mr Chase turned the gloss back into Syriac, and then looked for the scriptural words which in other places most closely agreed with the language of the glossator. The rest of his identification is equally devoid of force.

For, be it observed, *the gloss does not belong* in the last sentence of the vith chapter of the Acts at all, but in the next sentence at the beginning of the viith chapter: where the Bezan text is

---

[1] *Stud. u. Krit.* 1894, p. 115, "anschaulicher als in a"

ειπεν δε ο αρχιερεγc τω Στεφανω
ait autem pontifex Stephano.

We proceed to show that the gloss belongs after the word αρχιερεγc in the Greek, and after *pontifex* in the Latin.

The words are added in the sense that 'the high-priest stood in the midst and said to Stephen'; we have the exact parallel in the language of the Gospel in Mark xiv. 60

καὶ ἀναστὰς ὁ ἀρχιερεὺς εἰς μέσον.

If then there has been assimilation, this must be the passage to which reference has been made. The situations are similar, and the language of the unglossed passage furnishes the requisite link with the passage from which the addition has been made[1]; Stephen before the high-priest has been equated with Christ before Caiaphas, and the judicial examination of the disciple has been coloured from that of his Lord.

So much being clear, it is also clear that (1) the Bezan Latin *is more archaic than the Bezan Greek*[2], for it has preserved the necessary *stans* where the Bezan Greek has followed the exigencies of grammar and replaced ἑστώς by ἑστῶτος; (2) that the expansion made by the Fleury text *angeli dei* is probably a later addition and not a part of the original Western gloss; (3) that the Bezan Greek and Latin (ἐν μέσῳ αὐτῶν) are nearer to the primitive form than the *inter illos* of the Fleury palimpsest and the Leabhar Breac; (4) that Mr Bernard was wrong in praising the Greek of the gloss as nearer to the source than the Latin; (5) that Prof. Blass was wrong in calling it a part of the primitive text; (6) that Mr Chase was wrong in the source which he assigned to the gloss and in everything he said about it; (7) that I myself am an idiot for not having seen all this sooner.

---

[1] The importance of this consideration seems often to have escaped Mr Chase; it is not sufficient to establish assimilation between passages after glossation; the assimilation must be found in nucleus before glossation; something must suggest it before it is made.

[2] Chase, p. 5. 'The formation of the Bezan Latin must be independent of and later in time than the formation of the Bezan Greek.'

So much being premised we have still to ask the question as to the language in which the gloss was made.

It appears from the Fleury text as if there had been more of the passage in S. Mark borrowed than now appears, or as if the assimilation had been carried further by some later hand. For we have instead of the blunt text of the edited Acts

εἶπεν δὲ ὁ ἀρχιερεύς

the longer form

et interrogauit sacerdos Stefanum,

where notice that both D and E (Cod. Laudianus) are in evidence for τῷ Στεφάνῳ, and that the text of Mark is καὶ ἀναστὰς ὁ ἀρχιερεὺς εἰς μέσον ἐπηρώτησεν τὸν Ἰησοῦν, λέγων·

[d interrogabat īhm dicens],

and further the Peshito shows signs of the existence of something answering to ἐπηρώτησεν. since it reads the opening sentence

ܟܠܪܐܠ ܕܝ. ܣܗܡܐ

= et interrogavit eum summus sacerdos.

The genesis of the passage seems, therefore, pretty clear.

But it may be asked, was not the gloss originally added in Syriac rather than in Greek or Latin? Possibly it may have been; but while there are some things which look like it, there are others which are doubtful. The strongest argument would be the replacement of the primitive ἀναστὰς by ἑστὼς which might easily have been accomplished through the Syriac ܩܐܡ; on the other hand the Syriac would almost certainly have broken up the participial construction; moreover we miss the ܐܘܬܒܐܪ in the Syriac where it must have been perfectly natural, and we notice also that the text of Mc. xiv. 60 has the equivalent of ἐν μέσῳ (as also the Diatessaron), and not the Bezan ἐν μέσῳ αὐτῶν. Probably Mr Chase can clear up the matter, now that we have given him the clue. I may remark that the displacement of glosses (of which this is our first instance) is more natural in Syriac MSS. than in Greek Codices, on account of the glosses being often written along the margin, vertically; this custom carries the gloss along so much of the margin that the risk of displacement is much increased. The occurrence of frequent displacement in the glosses is, therefore, a palaeographical feature which is more in harmony with Syriac originals than with Greek texts[1].

Our next passage shall be the difficult gloss in Acts xv. 29

αφ ωΝ ΔιαΤΗΡΟΥΝΤΕC ΕαΥΤΟΥC
ΕΥ πραΖαΤΕ ΦΕΡΟΜΕΝΟΙ
ΕΝ ΤΩ αΓΙΩ π̄Ν̄Ι ΕΡΡωCΘΕ

= a quibus conuersantes uos ipsos
bene agitis ferentes
in santo s̄p̄o ualete.

The gloss is more interesting than the previous one, on account of the antiquity of its attestation. It is found in Irenaeus and in Tertullian; and found in forms which suggest either a primitive difficulty or an initial roughness of translation.

Irenaeus has *ambulantes in spiritu sancto*, the Greek of the gloss being problematic[2], and Tertullian has either

rectante uos spiritu sancto,

or   vectante uos spiritu sancto,

either of which is conceivably correct, *vectante* being near to the Greek φερόμενοι, and *rectante* being a good representation of the idea of guidance which underlies the word.

The occurrence of three such distinct Latin forms shows, as we have said, that there was either a difficult word somewhere to be translated, which has met with varied treatment at the hand of translators; or that the first translator into Latin made a bad or obscure rendering, which others have had to emend.

[1] Note however that the occurrence of 'stans' in the Bezan Latin shows that the gloss was meant to go into the next line in the Latin: which almost implies that it had stood outside on the margin of a [Graeco-] Latin text.

[2] We are perfectly safe in reasoning from the existence of the gloss in the Latin to its existence in the Greek. But whether the Greek was ἀγόμενοι or φερόμενοι or περιπατοῦντες, we cannot, at present, undertake to say. Probably a comparative study of the Latin of Irenaeus with the extant Greek would throw some light upon the question.

What are we then to say of the gloss: is it a part of the primitive dual redaction; a sentence truly belonging to the first period of genesis of the document? Or is it an insertion resulting from the tendency of scribe or commentator?

I believe the first suggestion with a view to explaining the gloss was that which I made in my 'Study of Cod. Bezae,' that it was the attempt of a later hand to refine upon the obvious unspirituality and insufficiency of the Jerusalem Concordat.

No doubt such a feeling would exist, both amongst the more spiritual people, like the Montanists, and amongst the more anti-Judaic like the Marcionites. The former would naturally desire some reference to the Paraclete, the latter would resent an apostolical communication which so partially removed the yoke of Judaism from the religious world.

I am sorry, however, that I made this suggestion as to the need for reforming and expanding the Jerusalem decrees because it has misled my friend Mr Chase, who has adopted the reason given by me for the gloss, and endorsed it by a number of arguments which are, I am afraid, all wide of the mark. His language is as follows:

"The Old Syriac[1] has 'well-ye-shall-be, be strong in our Lord.' Probably the Bezan εὖ πράξατε (true text εὖ πράξετε) represents an Old Syriac reading 'well-be-ye.' But what of the Bezan interpolation? I believe that the desire to make the apostolic decree more spiritual led to the introduction into the Old Syriac text of a phrase from a Pauline epistle which dealt with the Judaistic controversy. See Gal. v. 18. 'But if in the Spirit led (ܡܬܕܒܪܝܢ) are ye, ye are not under the law'; and compare Rom. viii. 14, Jn. xvi. 13, Lc. iv. 1: 'There led him (ܕܒܪܬܗ) the Spirit into the wilderness'; it will be remembered that we saw reason to think that the context of this last passage suggested the gloss in v. 26[2]. The rendering of the Syriac 'led' by φερόμενοι is quite natural (see the use of the Greek word in Mc. xv. 22, John xxi. 18, Acts xiv. 13),

---

[1] He means the Peshito.
[2] We shall show, bye and bye, that this is a delusion.

especially as the Bezan scribe in translating Syriac glosses frequently avoids the most obvious Greek word. The choice of the word was *possibly* influenced by 2 Pet. i. 21 (where the Syriac has another word).

This suggestion as to the source of the gloss is strongly confirmed by the fact that Irenaeus (iii. 17) preserves another Pauline form of the gloss 'ambulantes in spiritu sancto' (Gal. v. 16). It would appear that in this passage Irenaeus, like Cod. E in v. 39, vi. 10, preserves an Old Syriac reading different from that implied in Cod. D. My position that these are Syriac glosses is confirmed by the fact that the Syriac Vulgate preserves yet another expedient for spiritualizing the decree. In place of the simple 'be-strong' ($\check{\epsilon}\rho\rho\omega\sigma\theta\epsilon$), it has the phrase (see above) 'be strong in our Lord.' With this compare Eph. iv. 15, ܩܘܡ ܚܝܠ This Bezan gloss....together with that preserved in Irenaeus, implies an Old Syriac version of the Pauline Epistles."

I have quoted this passage almost at length on account of the illustration which it furnishes of Mr Chase's methods. Of the whole of this imposing mass of arguments, the only thing that is correct is the statement, which might have been made in half a line, that $\phi\epsilon\rho\acute{o}\mu\epsilon\nu\omega\iota$ may conceivably be equated with the Syriac ܡܬܕܒܪܝܢ.

For the gloss does not belong where Mr Chase imagines and where I first thought it to belong, but is a part of the following sentence, describing the Apostolic Mission to Antioch. The current text of this passage is

οἱ μὲν οὖν ἀπολυθέντες κατῆλθον εἰς Ἀντιόχειαν,

with which we must compare the parallel passage (xiii. 4),

οἱ μὲν οὖν ἐκπεμφθέντες ὑπὸ τοῦ ἁγίου πνεύματος κατῆλθον εἰς Σελεύκειαν.

Accordingly, the sentence in Acts xv. 30 should run,

'So they were led by the Holy Spirit, and came down to Antioch.'

The gloss, inserted here, makes perfect sense; it is in fact merely an expansion, or, if you will, merely an explanation of ἀπολυθέντες. There is no need to invoke Montanus or Marcion, or any anti-Judaic commentator, nor to make references to Galatians and parallels in Romans, John and Luke. Such references could not in any case have been in the mind of the glossator, unless indeed he were writing a sermon instead of transcribing a text.

Neither is there any reason to assume three separate forms of the Old Syriac in order to meet the exigences of the theory, one for Beza, and one for Irenaeus, and one for Tertullian[1]. Three separate Syriac origins, with perhaps a fourth for the Peshito, is rather a large order to explain so early a corruption. Neither is it necessary to explain the translation of the supposed Syriac word by φερόμενοι on the theory of translation by unlikely words, and a possible influence of 2 Pet. i. 21, where the Syriac has another word.

I am not quite sure whether I understand Mr Chase at this point. Does he mean that there was an Old Syriac text of 2 Peter? If so, he ought certainly to make a definite statement of his discovery of that lost text. But even so, he will still have to assign a reason why a passage from 2 Pet. should have any influence in the rendering of another passage in the Acts with which it is not in verbal agreement. If the reference to 2 Pet. is a good one, why is it not adequate to explain the gloss as from a Greek original? and does not the comment of Ephrem (p. 277) "ye shall receive the Holy Spirit to speak all tongues," imply the equivalent of a primitive φερόμενοι which has been interpreted as in 2 Pet. i. 21? It will be seen that we entirely dissent from Mr Chase's methods, but that is not the same thing as proving his theory invalid at every point, nor is it a reason for discarding it at all. Let us ask the question whether the gloss, as replaced in the sequence of Acts xv. 30, can be referred to its original language.

When we turn to the text of the Peshito, in the two passages which we have ventured to compare, we find the

[1] See the note on p. 95 of Chase. "It is quite possible that this (Tertullian's form) is to be traced to a Syriac gloss derived directly from Lc. iv. 1."

desiderated word ܡܬܪܒܐ in neither, nor any trace of the gloss in xv. 30. But we do find, and this is worthy of note, that the two passages are in harmony, as far as the principal verb is concerned, in the Peshito : compare Acts xiii. 4

ܘܗܢܘܢ ܟܕ ܐܫܬܕܪܘ ܡܢ ܪܘܚܐ ܕܩܘܕܫܐ
ܢܚܬܘ ܠܗܘܢ ܠܣܠܘܩܝܐ

and Acts xv. 30

ܗܢܘܢ ܕܝܢ ܕܐܫܬܕܪܘ ܐܬܘ ܠܗܘܢ ܠܐܢܛܝܟܝܐ

But whether any conclusion can be drawn from this we are not able to say. For the very same approximation of the accounts appears in Cod. Bezae which reads in xiii. 4

ipsi vero dismissi ab s͞p͞o sancto

and in xv. 30

illi quidem dismissi.

A translation from a richer language into a poorer vocabulary often results in an approximation of similar accounts : and as we have said, there does not seem any trace of the word ܡܬܪܒܐܢ which Mr Chase suggests : but perhaps this suggestion also is a mistake. Possibly Mr Chase may be able to find the traces of the missing or requisite word. We have no prejudice against his theory : for the sooner the problem is solved the better for all persons concerned.

Let us turn in the next place to the passage Acts v. 38, and see whether the supposition of a Syriac original will throw light upon the glosses, and in particular upon the curious gloss which appears in Cod. D in the form

ΜΗ ΜΙΑΝΑΝΤΕϹ ΤΑϹ ΧΕΙΡΑϹ
= non coinquinatas manus

and in Cod. E

ΜΗ ΜΟΛΥΝΟΝΤΕϹ ΤΑϹ ΧΕΙΡΑϹ ΥΜⲰΝ
= non coinquinantes manus vestras.

The passage is one to which I drew special attention (1) on

account of the appearance of an accusative absolute in the
Latin, which seemed to me to be original, (2) on account of
the coincidence between D and E in the verb used in the
Latin, although the Greek from which they were supposed to
be taken was different; I inferred that the gloss passed into
the Greek from the Latin.

The gloss certainly adds to the force of the narrative; and
so does the repetition of ἀποστῆτε ἀπ' αὐτῶν; and although
the two Greek forms cannot, of course, be original, that does
not mean that one of them may not be the original: and on
the other hand, neither of them need be original. If they do
not come from a primitive Greek or Latin, they may be, as
Mr Chase suggests, translations of a Syriac phrase. The coincidences between the two Latin forms would in that case be
accidental. On the supposition of a Syriac original, the first
thing that we should do is to look for any peculiarities or
irregularities conserved in the rendering of the Peshito. The
two verses (v. 38, 39) are as follows:

And now I say to you: Remove from these men, and let
them alone; for if this device and this work be from men, they
will dissolve and perish; but if it be from God, it does not
reach to your hands to annul it.

The reader will observe the curious translation of οὐ
δυνήσεσθε = ‏ܐܠ ܛܒܐ ܒܐܝ̈ܕܝܟܘܢ‎

If the gloss comes from the Syriac, I suspect that this
passage must be the cause of it; we have only to exchange two
letters, and read, with a slight change,

‏ܐܠ ܕܛܐ ܒܐܝ̈ܕܝܟܘܢ‎

to give the sentence "no pollution in your hands," which may
perhaps be recognized as an adequate original for the glosses in
the Western texts[1].

But if this explanation be correct, and it is the only one
which I can think of on the Syriac hypothesis, for Mr Chase's

---

[1] I do not spend time to prove that ‏ܛܐ‎ may rightly be rendered μιαίνω
or μολύνω or coinquino.

explanation seems to me quite impossible, then the gloss has again got into a wrong place in the text[1], as we saw in the two previous cases. If then the gloss be Syriac, we have drawn attention to three cases of displacement in the inserted glosses. We thus arrive at the conclusion that 'the glosses in the Codex Bezae show signs of having been inserted from the margin, either from the margin of the ancestry of the Codex or from the margin of some other Codex, the language of which Codex is not yet quite clear'; and further 'the displacement which is observable in certain of the glosses, is a strong though not a conclusive argument, against the theory that those glosses formed a part of a primitive redaction of the text.' Prof. Blass's theory will be much weakened if we can show that any of the glosses on which he relies are out of their true place. It is true that the theory of contamination of one of the forms of the primitive redaction by the other may help him to evade the difficulty; for if there were two primitive forms of the text, the second form (which Blass calls β, and which represents what Hort calls the Western text) does not exist unmixed, but, as we have it in D, in the form of an a-text contaminated by a β-text, or conversely; and this leaves open the possibility that sentences of the β-text may be wrongly affixed, as it can be shown that single words are often wrongly restored from some companion document. But it is doubtful whether this hypothesis would bear the strain of the cases of displacement which we are able to bring forward.

Returning to the gloss which we were just now discussing, we do not think that the explanation given of the displacement is decisive in the same sense as in the two previous cases, where there is really no room for doubt. But it would seem to be much more natural to explain the added words in this way, than to translate the sentence back into Syriac as Mr Chase does, and then search for obscure parallels to the language in the Old Testament[2].

---

[1] Or rather it has moved away from its right place.

[2] Mr Chase's argument is "In Isaiah lix. 3 there occur the words 'your hands are defiled with blood.'...From this verse came, I believe, an Old Syriac gloss (=and do not defile your hands)." Credo, quia impossibile est. There is no motive to take either a transcriber or glossator into Isaiah.

Having now shown that certain of the glosses do not lend themselves to Mr Chase's elaborate explanations, nor to Prof. Blass's justifications, on account of their not standing where the explanations assume them to stand, we pass on to make a few remarks on the question of the assimilations of the text, as when one passage of the Acts is conformed to or expanded from another passage of the Acts or as when the text of the Acts is similarly expanded from the Gospels, the Diatessaron, the Epistles, the Prophets, the writings of Papias (in Syriac), and the like, according to Mr Chase's explanations.

The question between Blass and the rest of the critics really turns upon the extent to which assimilation can be detected in the supposed glosses: if they are merely textual parallelisms developed in a version, and projected back upon the original text, the position defended by Blass becomes a hopeless one. But here, also, much will depend upon the extent to which the corrupting influence can be proved to work ; it is quite possible that there may be an occasional assimilation in the text without our being obliged to condemn as non-original those many vivid historical and geographical details with which the Codex Bezae abounds. No assimilation will explain the tarriance at Trogyllium, the fright of the Philippian magistrates over the earthquake, the visit of S. Paul to Myra (to which Ramsay has drawn especial attention on account of its influence on the story of Paul and Thekla), or the statement that Paul spent the night somewhere on the way from Cesarea to Jerusalem. The geographical details must be original or else they are the work of a man who was thoroughly familiar with the navigation of the Levant[1] and the topography of the Holy Land.

But, then, on the other hand, it is quite possible that many of the apparently original details are due to assimilation. We have pointed out two trifling instances already. Let us take one of the most striking cases, the passing by Thessaly in Acts xvii. 15. The man who added it, if it is an addition, was a Levantine traveller. Was he the original writer of the book, or a later wanderer ?

[1] It is in such questions as these that Prof. Ramsay's criticism is so valuable and suggestive.

The added passage in Cod. Bezae is

ΠΑΡΗΛΘΕΝ ΔΕ ΤΗΝ ΘΕϹϹΑΛΙΑΝ
ΕΚΩΛΥΘΗ ΓΑΡ ΕΙϹ ΑΥΤΟΥϹ
ΚΗΡΥΞΑΙ ΤΟΝ ΛΟΓΟΝ

and we have shown that something like it was current in the Old Syriac.

The obvious parallel is Acts xvi. 6 where the current text is

Διῆλθον δὲ τὴν Φρυγίαν καὶ Γαλατικὴν χώραν, κωλυθέντες ὑπὸ τοῦ ἁγίου πνεύματος (D adds μηδενὶ) λαλῆσαι τὸν λόγον (D adds τοῦ θεοῦ) ἐν τῇ 'Ασίᾳ......παρελθόντες (D διελθόντες) δὲ τὴν Μυσίαν κατέβησαν (D κατήντησαν) εἰς Τρῳάδα.

The suggestion that the expansion in c. xvii. 15 was made by a reviser in D, under the influence of the parallel passage in xvi. 6, leads to the supposition that he found in his text which he was reproducing the word παρελθόντες and not the διελθόντες which now stands in the Codex Bezae. That is he was revising from what Blass calls the a-text. But this is too hasty a conclusion, for the reviser, who is nothing if not a geographer, may be using the word παρῆλθον because he wishes to imply that St Paul went to Athens by sea (as we may be morally certain that he did go), and so did not go through Thessaly, but coasted by it[1].

The precision of the language is such that it seems difficult to ascribe it to a translator, who is merely incorporating an assimilation in a Syriac or other version. And this same precision of geographical knowledge seems to come out in the counter-change in Acts xvi. 6 where the D text substitutes διελθόντες because he imagines St Paul to have gone through Mysia. Here again the change is so delicate that it hardly seems likely that casual retranslations from the Latin or Syriac could effect so much[2].

[1] Hence Prof. Ramsay is perhaps incorrect in saying (*Church in the Roman Empire*, ed. 3, p. 160) that the reviser did not observe that Paul probably sailed direct from the coast of Macedonia to Athens.

[2] Prof. Ramsay points out to me that "there was in reality no need for the latter change, because in the Travel-document διέρχομαι is used with an accusative of locality to indicate 'going from point to point along a road or over a country'

Moreover when we turn to the Syriac of Acts xvi. 6 we find

ܡܠܠܘ ܕܠܐ ܕܩܘܕܫܐ ܘܪܘܚܐ ܐܢܘܢ ܟܠܐܘ

ܡܢ ܢܦܩܘ ܘܟܕ (v. 8) .... ܒܐܣܝܐ ܕܐܠܗܐ ܡܠܬܐ

ܕܡܘܣܝܐ

"and the Holy Spirit forbade them to speak the word of God in Asia;...and when they came out of Mysia," and this construction, which has every appearance of being close to the original rendering (for it agrees with D in the insertion of the 'word *of God*' and implies the journey through Mysia in a form which certainly suggests dependence upon the text of D) can hardly furnish us with the material for the gloss in xvii. 15: for this gloss does not imitate the construction, nor take up the equivalent of τοῦ θεοῦ, nor translate the equivalent Syriac word into λαλῆσαι. It will be seen, therefore, that there is a good deal to be said against the hypothesis of Syriac assimilation. Was it then a Greek assimilation? This has more probability; the language is similar; the passage to which assimilation is made stands as in the *a*-text without any addition to τὸν λόγον; and it is possible that this may be the explanation. But I can believe that Blass would find it possible to defend the originality (and I may say the Lucanity) of the gloss on the ground that παρῆλθεν in Acts xvii. 15 could equally be taken in the sense of 'neglect Thessaly,' especially when the explanation was made that 'he was forbidden to preach the word to them.'

On the whole the examination of the passage leans rather to the side of Blass, and in favour of an original element in the Bezan text, than to the theory of a revision; and certainly there is little to be said in support of Chase's position. We must remember, also, in dealing with these parallel passages, that Luke is a writer who repeats himself occasionally *with variations*,

in the performance of one's purpose, viz. preaching. This construction is found only in the Travel-document and in 1 Cor. xvi. 5—and nowhere else in Greek. Luke uses διέρχ. διὰ or κατά. .εὐαγγελιζόμενος both in the Gospel and in Acts i—xii In contrast to this παρῆλθον means 'neglect' 'leave unevangelized,' without laying any stress on the topography of the journey. The narrator of the Acts has never the faintest interest in topography and geography: he thinks only of the missionary character of the journey."

so as often to suggest a double use of some source, or the existence of a document which has been translated. One has only
to compare two such passages as Acts ii 44 sqq. and Acts iv. 32
to see what I mean. One account has καὶ εἶχον ἅπαντα κοινά,
the other ἀλλ' ἦν αὐτοῖς πάντα κοινά ; one account says καὶ
διεμέριζον, the other καὶ διεδίδετο ; one account has πᾶσι,
the other ἐνὶ ἑκάστῳ ; while they both agree in the expression καθότι ἄν τις χρείαν εἶχεν. What are we to say to
this ? is it the twofold use of some primitive document, or is it
the natural variation of a writer recording similar phenomena
twice over ? If it is the latter, then we must not be hasty in
assuming assimilations nor in determining their origin. For
Luke repeats himself with slight variations[1]. So much may be
said on behalf of Blass's theory.

Resuming now our discussion of the subject from Mr Chase's
point of view, we shall show briefly and rapidly that, as in the
case of the glosses, Mr Chase interprets the assimilations
wrongly, and assigns incorrect and unnecessarily obscure origins
to them, in those cases where a theory of Syriac assimilation
is most plausible.

I am going to draw his attention to what I consider to be
the best example extant of a Syriac assimilation in the text
of the Acts: and then to ask him to compare his own theory
of the genesis of the error, and see if he adheres to it. The
passage is Acts xv. 26 which stands in the Codex Bezae

ΠΑΡΑΔΕΔΩΚΑϹΙΝ ΤΗΝ ΨΥΧΗΝ ΑΥΤΩΝ
ΥΠΕΡ ΤΟΥ ΟΝΟΜΑΤΟϹ ΤΟΥ ΚΥ ΗΜΩΝ ΙΗΥ ΧΡΥ
ΕΙϹ ΠΑΝΤΑ ΠΕΙΡΑϹΜΟΝ.

The gloss is in the last line; it should come a line higher up,

---

[1] Compare also the case which we discussed previously where xiii. 4 and
xv. 30 are contrasted and note the variation in the similar accounts. Observe
further that the reviser (if he be different from the author) can be proved not
to make his assimilations in a *verbatim* manner. Take the great gloss, for
instance, which the Heraclean margin has preserved for us in Acts xxv. 24, and
compare such sentences as "dicebam ut sequeretur me in Caesaream ubi
custodiebatur ..quum autem dicerem, Vis judicari cum iis Hierosolymae," with
the parallels in the received text, and it will be seen how freely the author of
these sentences handles his materials. Assimilation does not mean agreement.

but that does not sensibly affect the sequence of the passage. The necessity for a gloss arose from the ambiguity of the translated word ΠΑΡΑΔΕΔωΚΑϹΙΝ, which would be much better for a word or two of explanatory matter. In the present case the source of the gloss is not obscure ; it is due to the influence of a famous passage in Sirach ii. 1: "My son, if thou draw near to the service of the Lord, prepare thy soul for temptation," which the Syriac renders

"thou hast surrendered thy soul to all temptations."

$$\text{ܡܘܣܝܢ ܠܟܠ ܢܦܫܟ ܐܫܠܡܬ}$$

Everything would seem to be adequate for the calling up of the gloss: it was necessary to add something for clearness; and the rendering of the text in Acts ܐܫܠܡܘ ܢܦܫܬܗܘܢ was sufficient to make the connexion at once with the famous verse in Sirach[1].

Mr Chase's solution of the passage is as follows :

"What of the gloss εἰς πάντα πειρασμόν which is also found in Cod. E ? The only other passage in the N. T. where the expression 'every temptation' occurs is Lc. iv. 13 συντελέσας πάντα πειρασμόν. In this latter passage, the Syriac Vulgate has 'all-of-them his-temptations,' but the Arabic Tatian 'cum consummasset diabolus omnem tentationem' (Ciasca, p. 8) is good evidence that the Old Syriac had a literal translation of the Greek. In the Greek there is no point of contact between Lc. iv. 13 and Acts xv. 26. But in the Syriac it will be noticed that ܫܠܡ = συντελέσας; in Acts ܐܫܠܡ = παραδεδώκασι; the same verb, that is, is used in the two passages though not in the same sense. I would suggest, therefore, that, when some Syriac scribe wished to qualify the words 'men who surrendered their soul,' the sound of the verb carried his thoughts to Lc. iv. 13, therefore he appended the phrase 'to (ܠ) every-temptation[2].'"

---

[1] A verse by-the-bye which is the heading of a famous chapter in the *Imitatio Christi*. If the explanation be correct, it is in evidence for the early translation of Sirach.

[2] The ܠ is, of course, not in the Syriac of Luke!

It is a hard exercise of faith to be told to connect two such unlike situations by means of the sound of a single ambiguous word which is admitted to be used in two opposite senses! We will make Mr Chase a present of our interpretation, for the better propagation of his theory. His assimilation to the Gospel is a false assumption, and must be abandoned.

It would also be wise to remove from his pages such cases as make the prophets of the Old Testament responsible for ordinary turns of speech in Syriac. For example, Acts vii. 43 appears in the ordinary text as

$$\kappa\alpha\grave{\iota} \ \mu\epsilon\tau\omicron\iota\kappa\iota\hat{\omega} \ \acute{\upsilon}\mu\hat{\alpha}\varsigma \ \acute{\epsilon}\pi\acute{\epsilon}\kappa\epsilon\iota\nu\alpha \ \mathrm{B}\alpha\beta\upsilon\lambda\hat{\omega}\nu\omicron\varsigma,$$

which the Codex Bezae, as far as we can judge, altered into

$$\acute{\epsilon}\pi\grave{\iota} \ \tau\grave{\alpha} \ \mu\acute{\epsilon}\rho\eta \ \mathrm{B}\alpha\beta\upsilon\lambda\hat{\omega}\nu\omicron\varsigma$$
$$= \text{in illas partes Babylonis.}$$

The passage is an interesting one, because the peculiar word $\acute{\epsilon}\pi\acute{\epsilon}\kappa\epsilon\iota\nu\alpha$ inspires confidence, and is the very word used in the LXX. of Amos v. 27, from which the quotation comes. If it is not genuine, we should have a prophetical assimilation indeed, but on the wrong side of the house and, as far as Mr Chase is concerned, in the wrong tongue! But it must surely be genuine.

Now Mr Chase suggests that $\acute{\epsilon}\pi\grave{\iota} \ \tau\grave{\alpha} \ \mu\acute{\epsilon}\rho\eta$ is a re-translation of a Syriac ܐܬܪܘܬܐ ܕܒܒܠ, and under the influence of a number of passages in the prophets. No one could I suppose object to a translation of the name of a country which either in Syriac or in Latin took the form *in partes Babylonis*. The idiom is sufficiently common in both languages. It occurs constantly in Syriac, at all events, and here are a couple of cases from the recently published Commentary of Ephrem on the Pauline Epistles:

1 Cor. xi. 16: nos, in partibus nimirum Syriae,
talem consuetudinem non habemus,

where the idiom is Ephrem's own = we Syrians; and

2 Cor. i. 8: de tribulatione nostra, quae facta
est in partibus Asiaticorum,

where the idiom is that of the primitive translator of the Pauline epistles, rendering ἐν τῇ 'Ασίᾳ.

Surely we need not spend time in proving further that either in Syriac or in Latin *in partes Babylonis* is idiomatic. Now let us transcribe Mr Chase's explanation, p. 73:

"The Vulgate Syriac does not help us; it has the phrase used in the Syriac of Amos v. 27 (comp. Matt. viii. 30, 2 Cor. x. 16). It is, however, through the Syriac that a solution of the problem comes. The word ܐܬܪܐ (= the place) is used to translate τὰ μέρη in Matt. ii. 22, xvi. 13 by the Old and Vulgar Syriac, and by the latter version (the Curetonian fragments here failing us) in Mc. viii. 10. In Acts ii. 10, xix. 1, xx. 2 the same Greek phrase is represented by ܐܬܪܘܬܐ (= the places). But this word 'places' takes us back to a series of passages in the Prophets: Jer. viii. 3 'all the residue...which remain in all the *places* whither I have driven them,' Jer. xxiv. 9, xxix. 14, xl. 12 'then all the Jews returned out of all *places* whither they were driven,' Ezek. xxxiv. 12 'I will deliver them out of all *places* whither they have been scattered in the cloudy and dark day.' Thus in the Prophets of the Captivity 'the places' is almost a technical expression meaning 'the foreign countries of exile[1].' The Syriac O. T. has ܐܬܪܘܬܐ in all these passages (comp. Jer. xlv. 5, Amos iv. 6) except Jer. xxix. 14 where the Syriac is varied, possibly because the word in the singular occurs later in the verse ('I will bring you again unto *the place* whence I caused you to be carried away captive'). We may therefore with some confidence believe that the Old Syriac read in Acts vii. 43 ܐܬܪܘܬܐ ܕܒܒܠ (to-the-places of-Babylon) and we can see the rationale of the reading. The Old Syriac is *more suo* harmonising, embellishing a quotation from one Prophet with a characteristic expression of other Prophets who deal with the same subject of the exile."

I forbear to criticise a passage where I can only praise the industry of the author; I am afraid it will offend Syriac

---

[1] I suppose like 'in partibus' in ecclesiastical circles for 'in partibus infidelium'!

scholars, and prejudice them against the theory which Mr Chase is propounding, and indeed I doubt whether a single one of the many references to the Syriac Old Testament which he detects, either here or elsewhere, will be accepted.

There are, no doubt, passages which will lend themselves to elucidation on the hypothesis of glossing in and from the Syriac; and there are passages which will not do anything of the kind. We have done something, in the foregoing argument, to remove obstacles from the pathway of Mr Chase's readers: but the more we think of it, the more complex does the Bezan text become. It has passed through the hands of a number of people of active mind, whose remarks are stratified in the Western text; they are not all of them Syrians; and it is not yet even proved that there are no Western expansions which are original. The whole history of the text requires renewed and careful inquisition, without prejudice in favour of the solvent power of a single hypothesis.

I shall conclude my discourse, in the interests of poetical justice, by showing that there is one important gloss in the Acts which Mr Chase was unable to explain, and which does not seem to yield to any theory except that of a primitive Latin reaction.

In Acts iv. 31, we have in the Codex Bezae

ΚΑΙ ΕΛΑΛΟΥΝ ΤΟΝ ΛΟΓΟΝ ΤΟΥ ΘΥ ΜΕΤΑ ΠΑΡΡΗΣΙΑΣ
ΠΑΝΤΙ ΤΩ ΘΕΛΟΝΤΙ ΠΙΣΤΕΥΕΙΝ,

= et loquebantur uerbum $\overline{\text{di}}$ cum fiducia
omni uolenti credere.

The gloss is an old one, occurring in Irenaeus, both in Greek and Latin, and in a less pronounced form in Augustine, who omits the last word.

Its origin is evidently an attempt to assimilate the fulfilment of the prayer to the prayer itself which is in v. 29

ΜΕΤΑ ΠΑΣΗΣ ΠΑΡΡΗΣΙΑΣ ΛΑΛΕΙΝ ΤΟΝ ΛΟΓΟΝ ΣΟΥ
cum fiducia omni loqui uerbum tuum.

Hence we expect naturally the addition of πάσης, and a number of MSS. show it. (For example, the Gigas reads

loquebantur verbum dei cum omni fiducia.) This is the cause
of the *omni* at the beginning of the gloss: but this *omni*
separated from *fiducia* by the line division has been read as a
dative, and turned back into Greek as πάντι with the result
that it has itself become the subject of expansion, in order
to limit the extravagance of the statement and to round off
the sentence. (The Syriac, of course, has no parallel phenomena; it cannot translate παρρησία except by a circumlo-
cution, nor, when it does translate, can it make any distinction
between παρρησία and πᾶσα παρρησία.) Such is, we believe,
the origin of the gloss. But as we have used so much
παρρησία in explaining to other people the errors into which
they have fallen, we must also promise to be modest, and to
retract this opinion, and any others which we hold, as soon as a
better explanation can be offered, and we can fairly be shown
to have made an erroneous statement [1].

---

[1] In the foregoing remarks I have avoided the discussion of certain test
passages which Mr Chase considers decisive, because they are not, at all events
as presented by him, of the nature of proof. It is not fair, for example, to
quote the reading "their sons and their daughters" in Acts ii. 17, in proof of a
Syriac origin of the Bezan text of the Acts, and to support the statement by
reference to Tertullian (*adv. Marc.* v. 8), without at the same time informing the
reader that Tertullian is expressly, and from the necessities of the case, quoting
Joel against Marcion, and that the Bezan text shows signs of having been
corrected to the text of Joel! The argument needs re-statement, to say the
least.

NOTE.

ON A POSSIBLE CONNEXION BETWEEN CHRYSOSTOM AND EPHREM.

The foregoing pages have been largely occupied with a discussion of the character of the text of the Acts which underlies the commentary of Ephrem, some of whose fragments we have collected from the Venice Catena. And it has been shown that the text upon which Ephrem was working was a text which, at all events in the latter half of the book, was closely related to that of the Codex Bezae.

We are now going to ask the question whether the lost commentary of Ephrem has had any effect upon the extant commentary of Chrysostom; did Chrysostom know Ephrem's commentary, either in Syriac or by a translation, and was he under the influence of it? The question is interesting, not only on account of the explanation which it may possibly furnish of certain textual phenomena in Chrysostom's writings, but also because there has been a wide-spread suspicion of some foreign element in Chrysostom's commentary on the Acts. Many scholars have gone so far as to deny that the work is rightly ascribed to Chrysostom, on account of the repetitions and other literary imperfections which characterise it; and while, on the other hand, a comparison of the general method of interpretation with that employed on the Pauline epistles would seem to justify the belief in a common authorship, there still remains the suspicion which is provoked by the internal evidence of the commentary, which leads us to say that it cannot be wholly due to Chrysostom, and certainly not to Chrysostom at his smoothest and best.

Now it will be interesting to see whether the Venice Catena throws any light upon the question of authorship suggested in the foregoing remarks. It will not be easy to draw conclusions from the study of a Catena which is largely made up out of Ephrem and Chrysostom, on account of the confusions and errors to which Catenae are peculiarly liable. If, for example, we were to remark that a certain section was ascribed to both Ephrem and Chrysostom, we should not be justified in assuming that the Catenist found similar matter in the commentaries of both writers, and therefore assigned a double authorship; for, in the first place, it is not an uncommon thing for a Catenist to dovetail together extracts from different writers; and in the next place, we have no collateral evidence for Ephrem's Commentary to which we can appeal in order to show that the Catenist's ascription of authorship is correct. Unless we can find, then, cumulative evidence of a number of passages ascribed to Ephrem-Chrysostom, of which the whole matter is substantially Chrysostom, we can hardly argue that there was common matter in the two commentaries.

Nor would the difficulty be much less in cases which were ascribed to Ephrem alone, but which were shown, by a reference to the printed text, to belong to Chrysostom. The heading might be an error of the original Catenist or one of his transcribers. So that we should again demand cumulative evidence, before we could discard the suggestion of error in the titles, and say, this passage is both Ephrem (as is proved from the Armenian Catena) and Chrysostom as is shown by his printed works.

Probably the best test would be to examine the Commentary of Chrysostom for evidence of another biblical text underlying his remarks, which should not only differ from his own text upon which the remarks are ostensibly made, but should agree with the text of Ephrem, or, which is the same thing, with those peculiar features of the Bezan text which we have shown to characterise the text of Ephrem. If such an analysis led to a satisfactory conclusion, we could then with some confidence go over the sections which had a double ascription, and those which seemed to have an incorrect ascription, and perhaps justify the headings in doubtful cases.

The following remarks are meant to suggest the line which such an enquiry should take. We will begin by examining Chrysostom's remarks on certain passages (in which our references are made to Savile's edition).

p. 845 (c. xix. 21) ἔθετο ὁ Παῦλος ἐν τῷ πνεύματι διελθὼν τὴν Μακεδονίαν καὶ Ἀχαΐαν, πορεύεσθαι εἰς Ἱεροσόλυμα. The text is the current one, but Chrysostom goes on οὐκ ἔτι ἀνθρωπίνως ἐνταῦθα ποιεῖ, ἀλλὰ πνεύματι ᾧ καὶ προείλετο διελθεῖν. The suggestion that Paul had at one time been wishing to act ἀνθρωπίνως, in his prospect of the journey to Jerusalem, takes us back to the gloss at the beginning of the chapter (Acts xix. 1) where the Bezan text tells us

ΘΕΛΟΝΤΟΣ ΔΕ ΤΟΥ ΠΑΥΛΟΥ
ΚΑΤΑ ΤΗΝ ΙΔΙΑΝ ΒΟΥΛΗΝ
ΠΟΡΕΥΕΣΘΑΙ ΕΙΣ ΙΕΡΟΣΟΛΥΜΑ,

aud the Armenian Catena expressly assigns this peculiar reading to the text of Ephrem. We must therefore say that, es the demonstration has already been clearly made of the agreement of the Ephrem text with that of Cod. Bezae, we have traces of an acquaintance of Chrysostom with a famous Bezan-Ephrem reading. There is no question here of an error in the heading of the Armenian Catena. The commentary, then, made by Chrysostom belongs to the Ephrem-text rather than to his own.

If now we keep before our minds the term which Chrysostom uses (ἀνθρωπίνως) to describe the action of Paul when he plans in his own will and has to be restrained by the Spirit, we can throw some light on the following passage, p. 816 (c. xvii. 14) ὡς ἐπὶ τὴν θάλασσαν· ὑπέμενον δὲ ὅ τε Σίλας καὶ ὁ Τιμόθεος ἐκεῖ. Ὅρα αὐτὸν καὶ ὑποχωροῦντα καὶ ἐνιστάμενον καὶ πολλὰ ἀνθρωπίνως ποιοῦντα.

The passage is one in which the Bezan glossator has told us that Paul was acting under the peculiar restraint of the Spirit,

ΠΑΡΗΛΘΕΝ ΔΕ ΤΗΝ ΘΕΣΣΑΛΙΑΝ
ΕΚΩΛΥΘΗ ΓΑΡ ΕΙΣ ΑΥΤΟΥΣ
ΚΗΡΥΞΑΙ ΤΟΝ ΛΟΓΟΝ.

It is implied, as a comparison with parallel passages shows, that Paul had been planning to do something else than go to Athens: he had been acting ἀνθρωπίνως. And Chrysostom points out what he had been doing; he had been *retreating* and *pressing forward;* now if we refer to Ephrem's remarks on this passage, we shall find that Chrysostom's word ὑποχωρῶν exactly corresponds to 'giving way' or 'receding' which we detected in the extract of Ephrem; and it was shown, also, that at this very point Ephrem must have had the Bezan gloss quoted above.

Either then this word ὑποχωρέω is a part of Ephrem's commentary, in which case Chrysostom's use of that commentary is demonstrated; or it was a part of its text; in which case we have a second time shown that the Bezan-Ephrem text underlies the remarks of Chrysostom.

We will next show that certain remarkable Bezan additions were known to Chrysostom, for which we have not yet recovered the evidence of Ephrem. Take the case of the tears of Simon Magus, the antiquity of which gloss is, as Mr Chase has pointed out, demonstrated by Tertullian's allusion (*Simon Samarites.. frustra flevit*)[1].

Chrysostom says that his tears were merely formal; p. 714, Δέον ἀπὸ καρδίας μετανοῆσαι, δέον κλαῦσαι καὶ πενθῆσαι· ὁ δὲ ἀφοσιώσει μόνον τοῦτο ποιεῖ· εἰ ἄρα ἀφεθήσεταί σοι· τοῦτο εἶπεν, οὐχ ὡς οὐ συγχωρηθέντος ἂν αὐτῷ, εἰ ἔκλαυσεν κτέ. It is, therefore, certain that Chrysostom knew the tradition about Simon Magus' tears.

The importance of this piece of evidence is that we are almost obliged to equate the *frustra* of Tertullian with the ἀφοσιώσει of Chrysostom and to carry their equivalent into the Western text; now if this could be done through the Syriac ܘܠܐ ܟܦܬ ܠܗ (= *and he did not really care*), we could perhaps connect the Bezan reading by ܘܠܐ ܟܠܐ ܠܗ (= *and he did not cease*); we should thus find an original for the curious καὶ οὐ διελίμπανεν of the Bezan Codex. The question would then arise as to the primitive form and language of the gloss, which was extant originally in the sense that 'Simon Magus pretended to weep[2].'

By the foregoing instances, we have done something to prove that there underlies the Commentary of Chrysostom a glossed text of the Acts something like the Bezan-Ephrem text, and differing from the text that accompanies the commentary. Bearing this in mind, let us now turn to Chrysostom on Acts xviii. 19 (Savile, p. 831): he tells us

διὰ τοῦτο ἐκωλύετο εἰς τὴν Ἀσίαν ἐλθεῖν, πρὸς τὰ κατεπείγοντα οἶμαι ἐλαυνόμενος. ὅρα γοῦν ἐνταῦθα καὶ παρακαλούμενον αὐτὸν μεῖναι, καὶ οὐκ ἀνεχόμενον, ἐπειδὴ ἠπείγετο ἀπελθεῖν· οὐ μὴν ἁπλῶς αὐτοὺς εἴασεν, ἀλλὰ μετὰ ὑποσχέσεως.

---

[1] *De anima*, c. 34.

[2] The somewhat similar case is that of the peculiar description of Gallio's conduct (Acts xviii. 17, "Gallio cared for none of these things"), which appears in the Bezan Latin as

tunc gallio fingebat eum non uidere

and in the Fleury text as

et gallio simulabat se non uidere.

If we compare this with the extract of Ephrem, printed on p. 48 of the present tract, we find the words

" He did not choose to stay longer with them ; because whither he was concerned to go, thither he had to go. However he did not simply leave them, but with a promise that they should expect his coming by the will of God."

The exact coincidence both in thought and language between the two extracts is obvious ; but there is enough difference in the handling of the argument to show that we cannot correct the ascription of the Catenist from Ephrem to Chrysostom : on the other hand the sentence ὅρα γοῦν κτέ is exactly in Chrysostom's manner ; and we can only conclude that the two commentaries were substantially giving the same thoughts in the same language : and as we are clearly dealing here with commentary and not with text, this means that Chrysostom has been incorporating the idea of Ephrem.

Turn in the next instance to Chrysostom's note on xvi. 39 (p. 812):

φοβοῦνται ὅτι Ῥωμαῖοί εἰσιν, οὐχ ὅτι ἀδίκως ἐνέβαλον· καὶ ἠρώτησαν αὐτοὺς ἐξελθεῖν ἀπὸ τῆς πόλεως· χάριν ᾔτησαν ταύτην κτέ.

and a reference to Ephrem *in loc.* shows that the concluding words are either a gloss in the text, or borrowed from the commentary of Ephrem : " So then *we ask of you this favour*, depart from this city, lest the same men, etc."

But a reference to the Bezan text renders it tolerably certain that the words in question are merely an equivalent to the παρεκάλεσαν of the text : so that we are obliged again to conclude that Chrysostom has been borrowing from Ephrem.

Next let us compare p. 721 (c. ix. 4) :

ἀλλὰ τοῦτον μόνον ἐπήρωσε καὶ ἔσβεσεν αὐτοῦ τὸν θυμὸν τῷ φόβῳ ὥστε αὐτὸν ἀκοῦσαι τὰ λεγόμενα

where Ephrem's remark is (if we may trust the Catena), " With the light he blinded him and so frightened him and with awful fear of his glory he extinguished his rage " ; here, again, the dependence of Chrysostom on Ephrem seems to be established.

Our last instance shall be from p. 713 (c. viii. 19) :

πῶς οὖν, φησι, πνεῦμα οὐκ ἔλαβον οὗτοι; πνεῦμα ἔλαβον τὸ τῆς ἀφέσεως· τὸ δὲ τῶν σημείων οὔπω ἦσαν λαβόντες· καὶ ὅτι τοῦτο ἔστι, καὶ τὸ τῶν σημείων πνεῦμα οὐκ ἔλαβον, ὅρα πῶς ἰδὼν ὁ Σίμων προσῆλθε τοῦτο αἰτεῖν.

We notice here the curious distinction between the Spirit of grace and the Spirit of gifts, by which distinction Chrysostom tries to explain the fact that baptized persons had not received the Spirit. The expression which he uses, the Spirit of signs, is taken from Ephrem, as may be seen from the extract quoted on p. 41 ('they sent Peter and John that by their laying on of hands the Samaritans may receive the *Spirit of signs*').

Reviewing the instances which have been brought forward, we think a good case has been made out for the theory that the roughness of Chrysostom's commentary on the Acts is due, in part, to the fact that it is based upon the previously existing commentary of the great Syrian father.

ADDENDUM.

The Marcionite reading of Galatians iv. 27, referred to on p. 19 of the present work, will be found again, though in a less obvious form, in Ephrem's Commentary on the Diatessaron (p. 34, ed. Mösinger), as follows : 'Vide quomodo isti filii tui locum principalem acceperunt in Jerusalem, quae sursum est, matre nostra, quam laudamus (*more correctly* confessi sumus) quae Moysi apparuit in monte.'

www.ingramcontent.com/pod-product-compliance
Lightning Source LLC
Chambersburg PA
CBHW071947100426
42736CB00042B/2298